THE LAW OF SUCCESS

Revised and Updated

Volume I

NAPOLEON HILL

and the Napoleon Hill Foundation

Edited by Matthew Sartwell

RENAISSANCE BOOKS

Los Angeles

THE PRINCIPLES OF SELF-MASTERY

An Introduction to the Master Mind
A Definite Chief Aim
Self-Confidence
The Habit of Saving

Library of Congress Control Number: 2001095409
ISBN: 1-58063-204-1

10 9 8 7 6 5 4 3 2 1

Design by Susan Shankin
Typesetting by Michelle Lanci-Altomare

Published by Renaissance Books
Distributed by St. Martin's Press
Manufactured in the United States of America
First edition

DEDICATED TO

_____

ANDREW CARNEGIE

who suggested the writing of the course, and to

HENRY FORD

whose astounding achievements form the foundation
for practically all of the Seventeen Lessons of the course, and to

EDWIN C. BARNES

a business associate of Thomas A. Edison,
whose close personal friendship over a period
of more than fifteen years served to help me carry on
in the face of a great variety of adversities
and much temporary defeat met with in organizing the course.

CONTENTS

PUBLISHER'S NOTE

BEFORE EVERYTHING ELSE, NAPOLEON HILL WAS AN INSPIRING public speaker. The Law of Success, as Hill likes to remind us, began as a lecture series. It was tested before many hundreds of audiences and molded by their responses. In print it was issued piecemeal at first, in different editions with slightly differing formats. Like many great men who belong to an oral tradition, Hill was constantly, throughout his life, updating and modifying his ideas.

In reissuing *The Law of Success* we hope to reconcile Hill the developer of seminal ideas with Hill the presenter and interpreter. On one hand this edition presents Hill's ideas in their most complete, most comprehensive, and original form. It is true to the text, using all materials (pamphlets and addenda) ever published under the Law of Success title. At the same time, it is true to the man. We attempt to allow Hill to be as modern an author as if he were still among us.

We have accomplished the second goal in three ways. First, where there was repetition of ideas we selected the most comprehensive, adding marginal notes to explain variations. Second, we included other marginal notes that illustrate Hill's points with more modern examples. All marginal commentary in these volumes are set off in a different font and style. Finally—and this is the most delicate issue—we have treated the text itself as we would the text of a living author. When we felt that something was obscure or misleading because the author's language is idiosyncratic or archaic or because it might be construed as out of step with modern thinking, we have made minor changes. Also, where Hill digresses (as when talking about physics or psychology) to discuss theories that have since been revised, we have made minor revisions.

For anyone who has ever been moved or affected by Hill's ideas—and know it or not, most of us have—this edition will set the standard for decades to come.

We hope and believe that when Mr. Hill sits in our Master Mind group and gives us his take on the work we have done, he will express his hearty approval. (We rather expect he will cheerfully suggest further improvements.)

—The Publisher

PREFACE TO THE REVISED EDITION

UPDATING ONE OF NAPOLEON HILL'S MOST ENDURINGLY popular and helpful works is an intimidating task. *The Law of Success* was first published in 1928 as a set of eight volumes. Its reception was phenomenal. It won immediate endorsement from two former Presidents of the United States, as well as a legion of other prominent figures from all walks of life, including inventor Thomas Edison, business tycoon F. W. Woolworth, and labor leader Samuel Gompers.

Since then, in various forms, *The Law of Success* has been reprinted more than fifty times. The power and usefulness of its message endure. Napoleon Hill's name has been synonymous with success motivation for generations of Americans; his influence is reflected in the work of countless successors. Like Hill's other books, such as *Think and Grow Rich* and *Keys to Success*, this book has guided millions of people to discover and pursue what they want most from life. Readers familiar with those books will recognize some differences in Hill's ideas in this work, particularly in the number of key principles and in their wording, but the power and wisdom of Hill's ideas are clearly, unmistakably here.

Why, then, change anything about the book? Why tinker with success? Because, quite simply, Napoleon Hill's whole life was a process of discovery. He dedicated himself to uncovering the qualities and traits that made great individuals, and for more than forty years after the publication of *The Law of Success*, he continued to observe and interpret the lives of successful people. There was nothing static about his approach; he re-fined and clarified his ideas at every opportunity so that they would be more useful to his readers.

This new edition of *The Law of Success* attempts to continue that effort. New examples of the application of Hill's ideas have been added to show that those ideas remain just as important, just as useful as they ever were. When *The Law of Success* was first published in 1928, Hill wrote of an "age of greater opportunity," in which he believed that Americans had unprece-dented freedom to make of themselves what they would. The new material in this text shows that despite an ensuing depression and several wars, de-spite tumultuous political and cultural change, that age endures into the present and shows no sign of vanishing.

Much of the modern world would have astounded (and delighted) Napoleon Hill, who was born in backwoods Virginia during the presidency of Chester A. Arthur. Fax machines, the Internet, magnetic resonance im-aging, gene therapy: These were all still dreams in the minds of individuals when Hill passed away in 1970. But they represent exactly the kind of ex-citing innovation and progress he so passionately believed would come from dedicated human effort.

The trustees of the Napoleon Hill Foundation have ordered this new edition of *The Law of Success* with full confidence that it continues a long and proud tradition of pointing the way to personal achievement. It can do no more than that. Success in such a pursuit depends on your choices and your actions.

This volume is the first of four that will contain the entire revised text of *The Law of Success.* In it, you will learn of Hill's belief in the power of the human mind and of his deeply held conviction that each of us must dis-cover a clear purpose for our lives. These are the foundations of the pursuit of success. You will also learn of the importance of self-confidence in that pursuit and the necessity of conserving and marshaling your resources, no matter how you define success for yourself.

Later volumes will teach you other important lessons, such as leader-ship and imagination, accurate thinking and concentration, cooperation and learning from your mistakes. Together these four volumes will be the most complete and authoritative guide you will ever encounter to making the most of yourself and your efforts.

Success is not achieved by application of a simple three-step program. It depends on a fully coordinated, comprehensive plan of action that enlists all of your abilities. Devote yourself to understanding each of the four lessons in this book before you move on to the next. When you have completed Lesson Two, review Lesson One before beginning Lesson Three so that you refresh your understanding of the Law of Success. You will find as you progress that each subsequent lesson depends on understanding all those that have preceded it. It does you little good and potentially much damage to know how to use the accelerator of a car if you have forgotten how to steer or brake.

So resolve to make the most of the tremendous opportunity this course represents. Prepare yourself to alter the way in which you think about success and how it is attained. Hundreds of thousands of other men and women have improved their careers, fortunes, family life, and sense of themselves on the basis of the Law of Success.

You can, too.

—Matthew Sartwell

THE AUTHOR'S ACKNOWLEDGMENT
OF HELP RENDERED HIM
IN THE WRITING OF THIS COURSE

———————

THIS COURSE IS THE RESULT OF CAREFUL ANALYSIS OF THE LIFE work of over one hundred men and women who have achieved unusual success in their respective callings.

I have spent more than twenty years in gathering, classifying, testing, and organizing the Seventeen Lessons upon which the course is based. In this labor I have received valuable assistance either in person or by studying the life work of the following:

Henry Ford
Thomas A. Edison
Harvey S. Firestone
John D. Rockefeller
Charles M. Schwab
Woodrow Wilson
Darwin P. Kingsley
William Wrigley, Jr.
A. D. Lasker
E. A. Filene
James J. Hill
Edward Bok
Cyrus H. K. Curtis
George W. Perkins

Henry L. Doherty
George S. Parker
Dr. C. O. Henry
General Rufus A. Ayers
Judge Elbert H. Gary
William Howard Taft
Dr. Elmer Gates
John W. Davis
Captain George M. Alexander
(to whom I was formerly
an assistant)
Hugh Chalmers
Dr. E. W. Strickler
Edwin C. Barnes

Robert L. Taylor	Elbert Hubbard
(Fiddling Bob)	Luther Burbank
George Eastman	O. H. Harriman
E. M. Statler	John Burroughs
Andrew Carnegie	E. H. Harriman
John Wanamaker	Charles P. Steinmetz
Marshall Field	Frank Vanderlip
Samuel Gompers	Theodore Roosevelt
F. W. Woolworth	William H. French
Judge Daniel T. Wright	Dr. Alexander Graham Bell
(one of my law	(to whom I owe credit
instructors)	for most of lesson one)

Of the people named, perhaps Henry Ford and Andrew Carnegie should be acknowledged as having contributed most toward the building of this course, for the reason that it was Andrew Carnegie who first suggested the writing of the course and Henry Ford whose life work supplied much of the material out of which the course was developed.

Some of these men are now deceased, but to those who are still living I wish to make here grateful acknowledgment of the service they have rendered, without which this book never could have been written.

I have studied the majority of these people at close range, in person. With many of them I enjoy, or did enjoy before their death, the privilege of close personal friendship which enabled me to gather from their philosophy facts that would not have been available under other conditions.

I am grateful for having enjoyed the privilege of enlisting the services of the most powerful human beings on earth, in the building of the Law of Success course. That privilege has been remuneration enough for the work done, if nothing more were ever received for it. They have been the backbone and the foundation and the skeleton of American business, finance, industry, and statesmanship.

The Law of Success course epitomizes the philosophy and the rules of procedure which made each of these men a great power in his chosen field of endeavor. It has been my intention to present the course in the plainest and most simple terms available, so it could be mastered by very young men and young women, of high school age.

With the exception of the psychological law referred to in Lesson One as the Master Mind I don't claim to having created anything basically new in this course. What I have done, however, has been to organize old truths and known laws into *practical, usable form*, where they may be properly interpreted and applied by the workaday person whose needs call for a philosophy of simplicity.

In passing upon the merits of the Law of Success Judge Elbert H. Gary said: "Two outstanding features connected with the philosophy impress me most. One is the simplicity with which it has been presented, and the other is the fact that its soundness is so obvious to all that it will be immediately accepted."

The student of this course is warned against passing judgment upon it before having read the entire seventeen lessons. This especially applies to this introduction, in which it has been necessary to include brief reference to subjects of a more or less technical and scientific nature. The reason for this will be obvious after the student has read the entire seventeen lessons.

The reader who takes up this course with an open mind, and sees to it that his or her mind remains open until the last lesson is finished, will be richly rewarded with a broader and more accurate view of life as a whole.

A PERSONAL STATEMENT
BY NAPOLEON HILL

from the 1928 edition

SOME THIRTY YEARS AGO A YOUNG CLERGYMAN BY THE NAME OF Gunsaulus announced in the newspapers of Chicago that he would preach a sermon the following Sunday morning entitled, "What I Would Do if I Had a Million Dollars!"

The announcement caught the eye of Philip D. Armour, the wealthy packing-house king, who decided to hear the sermon.

In his sermon Dr. Gunsaulus pictured a great school of technology where young men and young women could be taught how to succeed in life by developing the ability to *think* in practical rather than in theoretical terms; where they would be taught to "learn by doing." "If I had a million dollars," said the young preacher, "I would start such a school."

After the sermon was over, Mr. Armour walked down the aisle to the pulpit, introduced himself, and said, "Young man, I believe you could do all you said you could, and if you will come down to my office tomorrow morning I will give you the million dollars you need." There is always plenty of capital for those who can create practical plans for using it.

That was the beginning of the Armour Institute of Technology, one of the very practical schools of the country. The school was born in the imagination of a young man who never would have been heard of outside of the community in which he preached had it not been for the imagination, plus the capital, of Philip D. Armour.

Every great railroad, and every outstanding financial institution and every mammoth business enterprise and every great invention, began in the imagination of some one person.

F. W. Woolworth created the five and ten cent stores plan in his imagination before it became a reality and made him a multimillionaire.

Thomas A. Edison created the talking machine and the moving picture machine and the incandescent electric light bulb and scores of other useful inventions, in his own imagination, before they became a reality.

After the Chicago fire, scores of merchants whose stores went up in smoke stood near the smoldering embers of their former places of business, grieving over their loss. Many of them decided to go away into other cities and start over again. In the group was Marshall Field, who saw, in his own imagination, the world's greatest retail store, standing on the same spot where his former store had stood, which was then but a ruined mass of smoking timbers. That store became a reality.

Fortunate is the young man or young woman who learns, early in life, to use imagination, and doubly so in this age of greater opportunity.

Imagination is a faculty of the mind that can be cultivated, developed, extended, and broadened by use. If this were not true, this course on the Seventeen Laws of Success never would have been created, because it was first conceived in my imagination, from the mere seed of an idea which was sown by a chance remark of the late Andrew Carnegie.

Wherever you are, whoever you are, whatever you may be following as an occupation, there is room for you to make yourself more useful, and in that manner more productive, by developing and using your imagination.

Success in this world is always a matter of individual effort, yet you will only be deceiving yourself if you believe that you can succeed without the cooperation of other people. Success is a matter of individual effort only to the extent that each person must decide, in his or her own mind, what is wanted. This involves the use of imagination. From this point on, achieving success is a matter of skillfully and tactfully inducing others to cooperate.

Before you can secure cooperation from others, before you have the right to ask for or expect cooperation from other people, you must first show a willingness to cooperate with them. For this reason the eighth lesson of this course, *the habit of doing more than paid for* [in a subsequent volume], is one which should have your serious and thoughtful attention. The law upon which this lesson is based, would, of itself, practically insure success to all who practice it in all they do.

Below, you will observe a Personal Analysis Chart in which nine well known people have been analyzed for your study and comparison. Observe this chart carefully and note the danger points which mean failure to those who do not observe these signals. Of the nine people analyzed seven are known to be successful, while two may be considered failures. Study, carefully, the reason why these two men failed.

Then, study yourself. In the two columns which have been left blank for that purpose, give yourself a rating on each of the Seventeen Laws of Success at the beginning of this course; at the end of the course rate yourself again and observe the improvements you have made.

The purpose of the Law of Success course is to enable you to find out how you may become more capable in your chosen field of work. To this end you will be analyzed and all of your qualities classified so you may organize them and make the best possible use of them.

You may not like the work in which you are now engaged.

There are two ways of getting out of that work. One way is to take but little interest in what you are doing, aiming merely to do enough with which to get by. Very soon you will find a way out, because the demand for your services will cease.

The other and better way is by making yourself so useful and efficient in what you are now doing that you will attract the favorable attention of those who have the power to promote you into more responsible work that is more to your liking.

It is your privilege to take your choice as to which way you will proceed.

Thousands of people walked over the great Calumet Copper Mine without discovering it. Just one lone man used his imagination, dug down into the earth a few feet, investigated, and discovered the richest copper deposit on earth.

You and every other person walk, at one time or another, over your "Calumet mine." Discovery is a matter of investigation and use of imagination. This course on the Seventeen Laws of Success may lead the way to your "Calumet," and you may be surprised when you discover that you were standing right over this rich mine, in the work in which you are now engaged. In his lecture "Acres of Diamonds," Russell Conwell tells us that we need not seek opportunity in the distance; that we may find it right where we stand! *This is a truth well worth remembering!*

AN EXERCISE IN COMPARISON

The Seventeen Laws of Success	Henry Ford	Benjamin Franklin	George Washington	Abraham Lincoln	
1. The Master Mind**	100	100	100	100	
2. Definite Chief Aim	100	100	100	100	
3. Self-Confidence	100	90	80	75	
4. Habit of Saving	100	100	75	20	
5. Initiative & Leadership	100	60	100	60	
6. Imagination	90	90	80	70	
7. Enthusiasm	75	80	90	60	
8. Self-Control	100	90	50	95	
9. Habit of Doing More Than Paid For	100	100	100	100	
10. Pleasing Personality	50	90	80	80	
11. Accurate Thinking	90	80	75	90	
12. Concentration	100	100	100	100	
13. Cooperation	75	100	100	90	
14. Profiting by Failure	100	90	75	80	
15. Tolerance	90	100	80	100	
16. Practicing the Golden Rule	100	100	100	100	
17. Universal Law**	70	100	100	100	
Average	91	92	86	84	

The nine people who have been analyzed above are all well known. Seven of them are commonly considered to be successful. Two are generally regarded as failures, but of very different sorts. Napoleon had success within his grasp but squandered it. Jesse James gained notoriety and some cash but little else except a very short life. Observe where they each attained a zero and you will see why they failed. A grade of zero in any one of the Laws of Success is sufficient to cause failure, no matter how high any other grade may be.

Notice that all the successful figures grade 100 percent on a Definite Chief Aim. This is a prerequisite to success, in all cases, without exception. If you wish to conduct an interesting experiment, replace the

Study this chart carefully and compare the ratings of these nine people
before grading yourself in the two columns to the right at the start and end of this course.

Napoleon Bonaparte	Helen Keller*	Eleanor Roosevelt*	Bill Gates*	Jesse James	Yourself Before	Yourself After
100	100	80	100	100		
100	100	100	100	0		
100	90	80	80	75		
40	75	80	100	0		
100	90	90	90	90		
90	70	80	80	60		
80	70	70	60	80		
40	85	90	100	50		
100	100	100	100	0		
100	95	80	70	50		
90	75	80	100	20		
100	100	80	100	75		
50	100	90	100	50		
40	100	90	90	0		
10	100	100	90	0		
0	100	100	75	0		
0	100	100	75	0		
67	91	88	89	38		

above names with the names of nine people whom you know, half of whom are successful and half of
whom are failures, and grade each of them. When you are through, grade yourself, taking care to see that
you really know what are your weaknesses.

* Helen Keller, Theodore Roosevelt, and Bill Gates replace Theodore Roosevelt, William Howard Taft,
Woodrow Wilson, and Calvin Coolidge in Hill's original chart.

** These more recently defined Laws were added to the original chart and scored by the editor.

—— Lesson One ——

An Introduction to

the Master Mind

TIME IS A MASTER WORKER

THAT HEALS THE WOUNDS

OF TEMPORARY DEFEAT,

AND EQUALIZES THE

INEQUALITIES AND

RIGHTS THE WRONGS

OF THE WORLD.

THERE IS NOTHING

IMPOSSIBLE WITH TIME!

Lesson One

An Introduction to the Master Mind

"You Can Do It If You Believe You Can!"

T HIS IS A COURSE ON THE FUNDAMENTALS of success. Success is largely a matter of adjusting one's self to the ever-varying and changing environments of life, in a spirit of harmony and poise. Harmony is based upon understanding of the forces constituting one's environment; therefore, this course is in reality a blueprint that may be followed straight to success, because it helps you interpret, understand, and make the most of these environmental forces of life.

Before you begin reading the Law of Success lessons you should know something of the history of the course. You should know exactly what the course promises to those who follow it until they have assimilated the laws and principles upon which it is based. You should know its limitations as well as its possibilities as an aid in your fight for a place in the world.

From the viewpoint of entertainment the Law of Success course would be a poor second to most any of the monthly periodicals of the "snappy story" variety that may be found upon the newsstands.

COMMENTARY

It has been said that Napoleon Hill and his philosophy of success have made more millionaires than any other person in history. It might equally well be said that Napoleon Hill inspired more motivational experts than any other man in history. Napoleon Hill was, and thirty years after his death continues to be, America's most influential motivational author and lecturer. That is partly due to the fact that he came to prominence at the beginning of the age of mass communications, but it is due in even larger part to the diligence he applied to the research upon which he based his seventeen principles that comprise the Law of Success.

It is practically impossible to find a motivational speaker who does not draw upon Hill's work. His influence can be seen in the writings of his early peers, Dale Carnegie and Norman Vincent Peele. Later, many successful authors and speakers such as W. Clement Stone, Og Mandino, Earl Nightengale, and Chicken Soup for the Soul author Mark Victor Hansen either worked directly with Napoleon Hill or with the Napoleon Hill Foundation. Echoes of Hill's principles can be seen in books by people as diverse as Jose Silva, Mary Kay Ash, Dr. Maxwell Maltz, Shakti Gawain, Wally "Famous" Amos, and Dr. Bernie Segal. Anthony Robbins, arguably the most successful motivational speaker of the last decade, has often cited Napoleon Hill as his inspiration, and bestselling author Steven Covey's 7 Habits of Highly Effective People can be found in the seventeen principles Hill wrote about seventy years earlier.

AN OVERVIEW

The course has been created for the serious-minded person who devotes at least a portion of his or her time to the business of succeeding in life.

I have not intended to compete with those who write purely for the purpose of entertaining.

My aim, in preparing this course, has been of a two-fold nature: first, to help you discover your weaknesses, and second, to help create a *definite plan* for bridging those weaknesses.

The most successful men and women on earth have had to correct certain weak spots in their personalities before they began to succeed. The most outstanding of these weaknesses that stand between men and women and success are *intolerance, greed, jealousy, suspicion, revenge, egotism, conceit, the tendency to reap where they have not sown, and the habit of spending more than they earn.*

All of these common enemies of mankind, and many more not here mentioned, are covered by the Law of Success course in such a manner that any person of reasonable intelligence may master them with but little effort or inconvenience.

You should know, at the very outset, that the Law of Success course has long since passed through the experimental state; that it already has to its credit a record of achievement that is worthy of serious thought and analysis. You should know, also, that the Law of Success course has been examined and endorsed by some of the most practical minds of modern times.

The Law of Success Lectures

The Law of Success course was first used as a lecture, and I delivered it in practically every city and in many of the smaller localities throughout the United States, over a period of more than seven years. During these lectures I had assistants located in the audiences to interpret the reaction of those who heard the lecture, and in this manner we learned exactly what effect it had upon people. As a result of this study and analysis many changes were made.

The first big victory of the Law of Success philosophy was gained when it was used as the basis of a course that trained three thousand men and women as a sales army. Few of these people had previous experience of any sort in the field of selling. Through this training they were enabled to earn more than $1 million for themselves and paid me $30,000 for my services, over a period of approximately six months.

The individuals and small groups of salespeople who have found success through the aid of this course are too numerous to be mentioned in this introduction, but the number is large and the benefits they derived from the course were definite.

The Law of Success philosophy was brought to the attention of the late Don R. Mellett, former publisher of the *Canton* (Ohio) *Daily News*, who formed a partnership with me and was preparing to resign as publisher of the *Canton Daily News* and take up the business management of my affairs when he was assassinated on July 16, 1926.

Prior to his death Mr. Mellett had made arrangements with Judge Elbert H. Gary, who was then Chairman of the Board of the United States Steel Corporation, to present the Law of Success course to every employee of the steel corporation, at a total cost of something like $150,000. This plan was halted because of Judge Gary's death, but it proves that the Law of Success is an educational plan of an enduring nature. Judge Gary was eminently prepared to judge the value of such a course, and the fact that he analyzed the Law of Success philosophy and was preparing to invest the huge sum of $150,000 in it is proof of the soundness of all that is said on behalf of the course.

Terminology

You will observe, in this general introduction, a few technical terms that may not be plain to you. Don't let this bother you. Make no attempt at first reading to understand these terms. They will be plain to you after you read the remainder of the course. This entire introduction is intended only as a background for the other sixteen lessons of the course, and you should read it as such. You should read this introduction many times, as you will get from it at each reading a thought or an idea which you did not get on previous readings.

In this introduction you will find a description of a newly discovered law of psychology that is the very foundation stone of all outstanding personal achievements. I refer to this as the Master Mind, meaning a mind that is developed through the harmonious cooperation of two or more people who ally themselves for the purpose of accomplishing any given task.

If you are engaged in the business of selling you may profitably experiment with this Law of the Master Mind in your daily work. It has been found that a group of six or seven salespeople may use the law so effectively that their sales may be increased to unbelievable proportions.

Life insurance is supposed to be the hardest thing on earth to sell. This ought not to be true, with an established necessity such as life insurance, but it is. Nevertheless, a small group of men working for the Prudential Life Insurance Company, whose sales are mostly small policies, formed a little friendly group for the purpose of experimenting with the Law of the Master Mind, with the result that every man in the group wrote more insurance during the first three months of the experiment than he had ever written in an entire year before.

What may be accomplished through the aid of this principle by any small group of intelligent salesmen who have learned how to apply the Law of the Master Mind will stagger the imagination of the most highly optimistic and imaginative person.

Bear this in mind as you read this introduction to the Law of Success course and it is not unreasonable to expect that this introduction, alone, may give you sufficient understanding of the law to change the entire course of your life.

COMMENTARY

> *As you read this book you will occasionally encounter a term such as* Master Mind *that has, in the years since Napoleon Hill coined the term, taken on a connotation that he never intended. Hill first published this work in 1927, a time when Freud and Jung were still developing the study of human psychology, and the terminology had not yet found its way into common usage. The now commonly accepted psychological term that comes closest to capturing what Napoleon Hill meant by the Master Mind is what Jung called the collective unconscious. But what Hill was describing goes beyond Jung's theory to include other concepts including Edward de Bono's techniques of lateral thinking and brainstorming, and many of the ideas behind modern management buzz-words such as Quality Circles, synergy, and thinking outside the box.*
>
> *Hill's term,* Master Mind, *may seem quaint to the modern reader, but for all the psycho-babble that is now part of everyday speech, there is no other term that encompasses all that Hill had in mind.*

Personalities

It is the personalities back of a business that determine the measure of success the business will enjoy.

Modify those personalities so they are more pleasing and more attractive to the patrons of the business and the business will thrive. In any of the great cities of the United States merchandise of similar nature and price can be found in scores of stores, yet you will find there is always one outstanding store which does more business than any of the others. The reason for this is that back of that store is someone who has attended to the personalities of those who come in contact with the public. People buy personalities as much as merchandise, and it is a question if they are not influenced more by the personalities with which they come in contact than they are by the merchandise.

COMMENTARY

Hill is prophetic in these paragraphs. His description of the importance of personality and service in business anticipates the growth of the service industries that have, by the end of the century, dominated the economy.

Service

Life insurance has been reduced to such a scientific basis that the cost of insurance does not vary to any great extent, regardless of the company from which one purchases it, yet out of the hundreds of life insurance companies doing business less than a dozen companies do the bulk of the business of the United States.

Why? Personalities! Ninety-nine people out of every hundred who purchase life insurance policies do not know what is in their policies and, what seems more startling, do not seem to care. What they really purchase is the pleasing personality of some man or woman who knows the value of cultivating such a personality.

Your business in life, or at least the most important part of it, is to achieve success. Success, within the meaning of that term as covered by this course on the seventeen laws of success, is "the attainment of your Definite Chief Aim without violating the rights of other people." Regardless of what your major aim in life may be, you will attain it with much less difficulty after you learn how to cultivate a pleasing personality and after you have learned the delicate art of allying yourself with others in a given undertaking without friction or envy.

One of the greatest problems of life, if not, in fact, the greatest, is that of learning the art of harmonious negotiation with others. This course was created for the purpose of teaching people how to negotiate their way through life with harmony and poise, free from the destructive effects of disagreement and friction which bring millions of people to misery, want, and failure every year.

NO MAN HAS

A CHANCE TO ENJOY

PERMANENT SUCCESS

UNTIL HE BEGINS

TO LOOK IN A MIRROR

FOR THE REAL CAUSE

OF ALL HIS MISTAKES.

With this statement of the purpose of the course you should be able to approach the lessons with the feeling that a complete transformation is about to take place in your personality.

You cannot enjoy outstanding success in life without power, and *you can never enjoy power without sufficient personality to influence other people to cooperate with you in a spirit of harmony.* This course shows you step by step how to develop such a personality.

Lesson by lesson, the following is a statement of that which you may expect to receive from the seventeen laws of success:

The Master Mind will outline the physical and psychological laws that underline these lessons.

A Definite Chief Aim will teach you how to save the wasted effort that the majority of people expend in trying to find their life work. This lesson will show you how to do away forever with aimlessness and fix your heart and hand upon some definite, well-conceived purpose as a life work.

Self-Confidence will help you master the six basic fears with which every person is cursed—the fear of poverty, the fear of ill health, the fear of old age, the fear of criticism, the fear of loss of love of someone, and the fear of death. It will teach you the difference between egotism and real self-confidence that is based upon definite, usable knowledge.

The Habit of Saving will teach you how to distribute your income systematically so that a definite percentage of it will steadily accumulate, thus forming one of the greatest known sources of personal power. No one may succeed in life without saving money. There is no exception to this rule, and no one may escape it.

Initiative and Leadership will show you how to become a leader instead of a follower in your chosen field of endeavor. It will develop in you the instinct for leadership that will cause you gradually to gravitate to the top in all undertakings in which you participate.

Imagination will stimulate your mind so that you will conceive new ideas and develop new plans that will help you in attaining the object of your Definite Chief Aim. This lesson will teach you how to "build new houses out of old stones," so to speak. It will show you how to create new ideas out of old, well-known concepts, and how to put old ideas to new uses.

Enthusiasm will enable you to saturate all with whom you come in contact with interest in you and in your ideas. Enthusiasm is the foundation of a pleasing personality, and you must have such a personality in order to influence others to cooperate with you.

Self-Control is the balance wheel with which you control your enthusiasm and direct it where you wish it to carry you. This lesson will teach you, in a most practical manner, to become "the master of your fate, the captain of your soul."

The Habit of Doing More Than Paid For is one of the most important lessons of the Law of Success course. It will teach you how to take advantage of the Law of Increasing Returns, which will eventually insure you a return in money far out of proportion to the service you render. No one may become a real leader in any walk of life without practicing the habit of doing more work and better work than that for which he or she is paid.

A Pleasing Personality is the fulcrum on which you must place the crowbar of your efforts, and when so placed, with intelligence, it will enable you to remove mountains of obstacles. This one lesson, alone, has made scores of Master Salesmen. It has developed leaders overnight. It will teach you how to transform your personality so that you may adapt yourself to any environment, or to any other personality, in such a manner that you may easily dominate.

Accurate Thinking is one of the important foundation stones of all enduring success. This lesson teaches you how to separate facts from mere information. It teaches you how to organize known facts into two classes:
the important and the unimportant. It teaches you how to determine
what is an important fact. It teaches you how to build definite working
plans, in the pursuit of any calling, based on facts.

Concentration teaches you how to focus your attention upon one subject at
a time until you have worked out practical plans for mastering that subject. It will teach you how to ally yourself with others in such a manner
that you may have the use of their entire knowledge to back you up in
your own plans and purposes. It will give you a practical working
knowledge of the forces around you and show you how to harness and
use these forces in furthering your own interests.

Cooperation will teach you the value of teamwork in all you do. In this lesson you will be taught how to apply the Law of the Master Mind described in this introduction and in Lesson Two of this course. This
lesson will show you how to coordinate your own efforts with those of
others, in such a manner that friction, jealousy, strife, envy, and greed will
be eliminated. You will learn how to make use of all that other people
have learned about the work in which you are engaged.

Profiting by Failure will teach you how to make stepping stones out of all
of your past and future mistakes and failures. It will teach you the difference between failure and temporary defeat, a difference which is very
great and very important. It will teach you how to profit by your own
failures and by the failures of other people.

Tolerance will teach you how to avoid the disastrous effects of racial and
religious prejudices which mean defeat for millions of people who permit themselves to become entangled in foolish argument over these

subjects, thereby poisoning their own minds and closing the door to reason and investigation. This lesson is the twin sister of the one on accurate thought for the reason that no one may become an accurate thinker without practicing tolerance. Intolerance closes the book of knowledge and writes on the cover, "Finis! I have learned it all!" Intolerance makes enemies of those who should be friends. It destroys opportunity and fills the mind with doubt, mistrust, and prejudice.

Practicing the Golden Rule will teach you how to make use of this great universal law of human conduct in such a manner that you may easily get harmonious cooperation from any individual or group of individuals. Lack of understanding of the law upon which the Golden Rule philosophy is based is one of the major causes of failure of millions of people who remain in misery, poverty, and want all their lives. This lesson has nothing whatsoever to do with religion in any form, nor with sectarianism, nor have any of the other lessons of this course on the Law of Success.

The Universal Law will show you how to apply the principles you have learned in studying the first sixteen lessons to transform not only your thoughts but also your habits. And through this change in the ways you behave and respond, you will put yourself in total harmony with your environment. Success is a result of achieving such harmony.

When you have mastered these seventeen laws and made them your own, as you may do within a period of from fifteen to thirty weeks, you will be ready to develop sufficient personal power to insure the attainment of your Definite Chief Aim.

The purpose of these seventeen laws is to develop or help you organize all the knowledge you have, and all you acquire in the future, so you may turn this knowledge into power.

You should read *The Principles of Self-Mastery* with a notebook by your side, for you will observe that ideas will begin to flash into your mind as you read, as to ways and means of using these laws in advancing your own interests.

You should also begin teaching these laws to those in whom you are most interested, as it is a well-known fact that the more one tries to teach a subject the more one learns about that subject. A parent with a family of young boys and girls may so indelibly fix these seventeen laws of success in their minds that this teaching will change the entire course of their lives. The parent with a family should interest his or her spouse in studying this course also, for reasons that will be plain before you complete reading this introduction.

Power is one of the three basic objects of human endeavor.

Power is of two classes—that developed through coordination of natural physical laws, and that developed by organizing and classifying knowledge.

Power growing out of organized knowledge is the more important because it places in your possession a tool with which you may transform, redirect, and to some extent harness and use the other form of power.

The object of this reading course is to mark the route by which you may safely travel in gathering such facts as you wish to weave into your fabric of knowledge.

There are two major methods of gathering knowledge, namely, by studying, classifying, and assimilating facts which have been organized by other people, and through one's own process of gathering, organizing, and classifying facts, generally called personal experience.

This lesson deals mainly with the ways and means of studying the facts and data gathered and classified by other people.

THE MASTER MIND AND THE
STRUCTURE OF THE UNIVERSE

In the past few centuries, scientists have discovered and catalogued the physical elements of which all material forms in the universe consist.

IF YOU MUST SLANDER SOMEONE,

DON'T SPEAK IT—BUT WRITE IT—

WRITE IT IN THE SAND,

NEAR THE WATER'S EDGE!

COMMENTARY

In the following pages, Hill explains basic laws of physics as they were understood in his time. There are errors in his understanding that will be recognized by even nonscientists. Hill, for example, says that electrons may be either positive or negative. An electron, we now know, always carries a negative charge. And a whole branch of physics studies particles much smaller than the electron, a world Hill hadn't an inkling of.

Where Hill digresses to discuss specifics, small sections have been deleted. Hill would have deleted them himself had he known more. But it is important to read the outlines of his description of physical matter as a metaphor or parallel for the laws that govern human behavior. That is the way he intended this section to be read. Hill is trying to find a physical basis to explain the extremely mysterious but altogether indisputable power of the Master Mind.

By study and analysis and accurate measurements humans have discovered the "bigness" of the material side of the universe as represented by planets, suns, and stars, some of which are known to be over ten million times as large as the little earth on which we live.

On the other hand, man has discovered the "littleness" of the physical forms that constitute the universe by reducing the physical elements to molecules, atoms, and, finally, to the smallest particle, the electron. An electron cannot be seen; it is but a center of force consisting of a positive or a negative. The electron is the beginning of everything of a physical nature.

Molecules, Atoms, and Electrons

To understand both the detail and the perspective of the process through which knowledge is gathered, organized, and classified, it seems essential to begin with the smallest and simplest particles of physical matter, because these are the ABCs with which Nature has constructed the entire framework of the physical portion of the universe.

The molecule consists of atoms, which are little invisible particles of matter revolving continuously with the speed of lightning on exactly the same principle that the earth revolves around the sun. These little particles of matter known as atoms, which revolve in one continuous circuit, in the molecule, are made up of electrons, the smallest particles of physical matter.

As already stated, the electron is nothing but two forms of force. The electron is uniform, of but one class, size, and nature; thus in a grain of sand or a drop of water the entire principle upon which the whole universe operates is duplicated.

How marvelous! How stupendous! You may gather some slight idea of the magnitude of it all the next time you eat a meal, by remembering that every article of food you eat, the plate on which you eat it, the tableware, and the table itself are, in final analysis, but a collection of *electrons*.

In the world of physical matter, whether one is looking at the largest star that floats through the heavens or the smallest grain of sand to be found on earth, the object under observation is but an organized collection of molecules, atoms, and electrons revolving around one another at inconceivable speed.

Nothing is ever still, although nearly all physical matter may appear, to the physical eye, to be motionless. There is no solid physical matter. The hardest piece of steel is but an organized mass of revolving particles. Moreover, the electrons in a piece of steel are of the same nature and move at the same rate of speed as the electrons in gold, silver, brass, or pewter.

The forms of physical matter appear to be different from one another, and they are different, because they are made up of different combinations of atoms (although the electrons in these atoms are always the same, except that some electrons are positive and some are negative, meaning that some carry a positive charge of electrification while others carry a negative charge).

Through the science of chemistry, matter may be broken up into atoms, which are, within themselves, unchangeable. The elements are created through, and by reason of, combining and changing of the positions of the atoms. Thus it may be seen that the physical elements of the universe differ from one another only in the number of electrons composing their atoms, and the number and arrangement of those atoms in the molecules of each element.

As an illustration, an atom of mercury contains eighty positive charges (electrons) in its nucleus and eighty negative outlying charges (electrons). If only the chemist were to expel two of its positive electrons it would instantly become the metal known as platinum. If only the chemist could then go a step further and transform the platinum into *gold!*

The formula through which this electronic change might be produced has been the object of diligent search by the alchemists all down the ages, and by the modern chemists of today.

It is a fact known to every chemist that literally tens of thousands of synthetic substances may be composed out of only four kinds of atoms, that is, hydrogen, oxygen, nitrogen, and carbon.

It may be stated as a literal truth that the atom is the universal particle with which Nature builds all material forms, from a grain of sand to the largest star that floats through space. The atom is Nature's building block out of which she erects an oak tree or a pine, a rock of sandstone or granite, a mouse or an elephant.

COMMENTARY

Hill is indicating here that the universe is filled with invisible untapped energy. It is the kind of energy that would later be demonstrated in the explosion of the first atomic bomb.

But the essential message of this example is this: Around a clump of matter there is a swirl of energy. That energy determines whether something attracts other objects or whether it repels them. The nature of this energy can allow two hydrogen atoms to bond with an oxygen atom to form a molecule of water, or a sodium and a chloride atom to join to create a molecule of salt. The nucleuses of the atoms are never changed, but the atoms themselves are joined into something new because of the nature of their energy.

In a Master Mind group, the energy of their individual minds surrounds the people who comprise the group. Their energies interact, and what results is something new and different.

These facts concerning the smallest analyzable particles of matter have been briefly referred to as a starting point from which we shall undertake to ascertain how to develop and apply the law of *power.*

Vibrating Matter

It has been noticed that all matter is in a constant state of vibration or motion; that the molecule is made up of rapidly moving particles called atoms, which, in turn, are made up of rapidly moving particles called electrons.

In every particle of matter there is an invisible force which causes the atoms to circle around one another at an inconceivable rate of speed.

One rate of vibration causes what is known as sound. The human ear can detect only the sound that is produced through from 20 to about 20,000 cycles per second.

As the rate of cycles per second increases above that which we call sound they begin to manifest themselves in the form of heat. Today this phenomenon is used in microwave ovens.

Still higher up the scale, vibrations or cycles begin to register in the form of light. Ultraviolet rays are normally invisible, and energy with a wavelength of higher order than ultraviolet is also invisible but can have a tremendous effect on physical objects. Science is still probing these upper limits and perhaps future discoveries will explain what today remains a mystery.

Yet still higher up the scale—just how high no one is able to say at this point—the vibrations or cycles create the power, I believe, with which humans *think.*

It's my belief that all vibration, out of which grow all known forms of energy, is universal in nature; that the fluid portion of light, the difference in effect between sound and light being only a difference in rate of vibration, also that of thought is exactly the same, as that in sound, heat, and light, excepting the number of vibrations per second.

Just as there is but one form of physical matter, of which the earth and all the other planets, suns, and stars are composed so is there but one form of energy, which causes all matter to remain in a constant state of rapid motion.

Dr. Alexander Graham Bell, inventor of the long distance telephone and one of the accepted authorities on the subject of vibration, is here introduced in support of my theories of vibration:

Suppose you have the power to make an iron rod vibrate with any desired frequency in a dark room. At first, when vibrating slowly, its movement will be indicated by only one sense, that of touch. As soon as the vibrations increase, a low sound will emanate from it and it will appeal to two senses.

At about 32,000 vibrations to the second the sound will be loud and shrill, but at 40,000 vibrations it will be silent and the movements of the rod will not be perceived by touch. Its movements will be perceived by no ordinary human sense.

From this point up to about 1,500,000 vibrations per second, we have no sense that can appreciate any effect of the intervening vibrations. After that stage is reached, movement is indicated first by the sense of temperature and then, when the rod becomes red hot, by the sense of sight. At 3,000,000 it

DON'T BE AFRAID

OF A LITTLE OPPOSITION.

REMEMBER THAT

THE KITE OF SUCCESS

GENERALLY RISES AGAINST

THE WIND OF ADVERSITY—

NOT WITH IT!

sheds violet light. Above that it sheds ultra-violet rays and other invisible radiations, some of which can be perceived by instruments and employed by us.

Now it has occurred to me that there must be a great deal to be learned about the effect of those vibrations in the great gap where the ordinary human senses are unable to hear, see or feel the movement. The power to send wireless messages by ether vibrations lies in that gap, but the gap is so great that it seems there must be much more. You must make machines practically to supply new senses, as the wireless instruments do.

Can it be said, when you think of that great gap, that there are not many forms of vibrations that may give us results as wonderful as, or even more wonderful than, the wireless waves? It seems to me that in this gap lie the vibrations that we have assumed to be given off by our brains and nerve cells when we think. But then, again, they may be higher up, in the scale beyond the vibrations that produce the ultraviolet rays.

[NOTE: The last sentence suggests my theory.]

Do we need a wire to carry these vibrations? Will they not pass through the ether without a wire, just as the wireless waves do? How will they be perceived by the recipient? Will he hear a series of signals or will he find that another man's thoughts have entered into his brain?

We may indulge in some speculations based on what we know of the wireless waves, which, as I have said, are all we can recognize of a vast series of vibrations which theoretically must exist. If the thought waves are similar to the wireless waves, they must pass from the brain and flow endlessly around the world and the universe. The body and the skull and other solid obstacles would form no obstruction to their passage, as they

RENDER MORE SERVICE

THAN THAT FOR WHICH

YOU ARE PAID AND

YOU WILL SOON BE PAID

FOR MORE THAN YOU RENDER.

THE LAW OF

INCREASING RETURNS

TAKES CARE OF THIS.

pass through the ether which surrounds the molecules of every substance, no matter how solid and dense.

You ask if there would not be constant interference and confusion if other people's thoughts were flowing through our brains and setting up thoughts in them that did not originate with ourselves?

How do you know that other men's thoughts are not interfering with yours now? I have noticed many phenomena of mind disturbances that I have never been able to explain. For instance, there is the inspiration or the discouragement that a speaker feels in addressing an audience. I have experienced this many times in my life and have never been able to define exactly the physical causes of it.

Many recent scientific discoveries, in my opinion, point to a day not far distant perhaps, when men will read one another's thoughts, when thoughts will be conveyed directly from brain to brain without intervention of speech, writing or any of the present known methods of communication.

It is not unreasonable to look forward to a time when we shall see without eyes, hear without ears and talk without tongues. Briefly, the hypothesis that mind can communicate directly with mind rests on the theory that thought or vital force is a form of electrical disturbance, that it can be taken up by induction and transmitted to a distance either through a wire or simply through the all-pervading ether, as in the case of wireless telegraph waves.

There are many analogies suggesting that thought is of the nature of an electrical disturbance. A nerve, which is of the same substance as the brain, is an excellent conductor of the electric current. When we first passed an electrical current through the nerves of a dead man we were shocked and amazed to see him sit up and move. The electrified nerves produced contraction of the muscles very much as in life.

The nerves appear to act upon the muscles very much as the electric current acts upon an electromagnet. The current magnetizes a bar of iron placed at right angles to it, and the nerves produce, through the intangible current of vital force that flows through them, contraction of the muscular fibers that are arranged at right angles to them.

It would be possible to cite many reasons why thought and vital force may be regarded as of the same nature as electricity. The electric current is held to be a wave motion of the ether, the hypothetical substance that fills all space and pervades all substances. We believe that there must be ether because without it the electric current could not pass through a vacuum, or sunlight through space. It is reasonable to believe that only a wave motion of a similar character can produce the phenomena of thought and vital force. We may assume that the brain cells act as a battery and that the current produced flows along the nerves.

But does it end there? Does it not pass out of the body in waves which flow around the world unperceived by our senses, just as the wireless waves passed unperceived before Hertz and others discovered their existence?

Every Mind Both a Broadcasting and a Receiving Station

More times than I can enumerate, I have proven to my own satisfaction at least, that every human brain is both a broadcasting and a receiving station for vibrations of thought frequency.

If this theory should turn out to be a fact, and methods of reasonable control should be established, imagine the part it would play in the gathering, classifying, and organizing of knowledge. The possibility, much less the probability, of such a reality, is staggering!

Thomas Paine was one of the great minds of the American revolutionary period. To him more, perhaps, than to any other one person, we owe both the beginning and the happy ending of the Revolution, for it was his keen mind that both helped in drawing up the Declaration of Independence and in persuading the signers of that document to translate it into terms of reality.

In speaking of the source of his great storehouse of knowledge, Paine thus described it:

Any person, who has made observations on the state of progress of the human mind by observing his own, cannot but have observed that there are two distinct classes of what are called thoughts: those that we produce in ourselves by reflection and the act of thinking, and those that bolt into the mind of their own accord. I have always made it a rule to treat these voluntary visitors with civility, taking care to examine, as well as I was able, if they were worth entertaining; and it is from them I have acquired almost all the knowledge that I have. As to the learning that any person gains from school education, it serves only like a small capital, to put him in the way of beginning learning for himself afterwards. Every person of learning is finally his own teacher, the reason for which is, that principles cannot be impressed upon the memory; their place of mental residence is the understanding, and they are never so lasting as when they begin by conception.

In the foregoing words Paine described an experience which at one time or another is the experience of every person. Who is there so unfortunate as not to have received positive evidence that thoughts and even complete ideas will pop into the mind from outside sources?

I believe that every thought vibration released by every brain is picked up by the ether and kept in motion in circuitous wavelengths corresponding in length to the intensity of the energy used in their release; that these vibrations remain in motion forever; that they are one of the

EVERY FAILURE IS A

BLESSING IN DISGUISE,

PROVIDING IT TEACHES

SOME NEEDED LESSON

ONE COULD NOT HAVE

LEARNED WITHOUT IT.

MOST SO-CALLED

FAILURES ARE ONLY

TEMPORARY DEFEATS.

two sources from which thoughts which pop into one's mind emanate, the other source being direct and immediate contact through the ether with the brain releasing the thought vibration.

Thus it will be seen that if this theory is a fact the boundless space of the whole universe is now and will continue to become literally a mental library wherein may be found all the thoughts released by human beings.

COMMENTARY

Imagine what a part this principle plays in every walk of life. You have probably experienced it with those you love, or with someone you work alongside. There you are, the both of you considering the solution to some problem, and you hit on the same idea at the same moment.

You have probably also noticed that the intensity of thoughts can increase their power to affect other minds. When you listen to a passionate speaker, don't you sometimes know what will be said next, even the words that will be used? This may sometimes be due to simple logical interpretation, yet it is just as likely to happen when you are hearing someone speak on something you know little about. In such a case, you have little basis for anticipating anything. Yet the power of the other person's thoughts conveys to you the ideas that are being expounded.

Imagine, then, applying this effect to your pursuit of success through harmonious and purposeful alliance of two or more minds. Two words are key here: harmonious *and* purposeful.

Organized Knowledge

I am here laying the foundation for one of the most important hypotheses enumerated in Lesson Three.

This is a lesson on organized knowledge. Most of the useful knowledge to which the human race has become heir has been preserved and accurately recorded in nature's Bible. By turning back the pages of this unalterable Bible we have read the story of the terrific struggle through and out of which the present civilization has grown. The pages of this Bible are made up of the physical elements of which this earth and the other planets consist, and of the ether that fills all space.

By turning back the pages written on stone and covered near the surface of this earth on which we live, we have uncovered the bones, skeletons, footprints, and other unmistakable evidence of the history of animal life on this earth, planted there for our enlightenment and guidance by the hand of Mother Nature throughout unbelievable periods of time. The evidence is plain and unmistakable. The great stone pages of nature's Bible found on this earth and the endless pages of that Bible represented by the ether wherein all past human thought has been recorded, constitute an authentic source of communication between the Creator and his creation. This Bible was begun before humankind had reached the thinking stage; indeed before life had reached the ameba (one-cell animal) stage of development.

This Bible is above and beyond our power to alter. Moreover, it tells its story not in the ancient dead languages or hieroglyphics but in universal language which all who have eyes may read. Nature's Bible, from which we have derived all the knowledge that is worth knowing, is one that no one may alter or in any manner tamper with.

The most marvelous discovery yet made is that of the recently discovered radio principle. Imagine picking up the ordinary vibration of sound and transforming that vibration from audio frequency into radio frequency, sending it to a properly attuned receiving station and there transforming it back into its original form of audio frequency, all in the flash of a second. It should surprise no one that such a force could gather up the vibration of thought and keep that vibration in motion forever.

The instantaneous transmission of sound, by means of the modern radio apparatus, makes not only possible but probable my theory—thought vibration can connect mind to mind.

COMMENTARY

Napoleon Hill wrote these words in 1927, a time of great optimism in America. The economy was booming, and advances in science and industry were happening so swiftly that it seemed to many people that nothing was impossible.

Needless to say, mind-to-mind communication did not happen in Hill's lifetime. However, if you take the extraordinary work being done at the beginning of the twenty-first century in communications technology and artificial intelligence, and combine it with the knowledge being gained about DNA and the human genome, it seems possible, perhaps even probable, that in some form Hill's theory of mind-to-mind communication will be realized.

The Master Mind

We come, now, to the next step in the description of the ways and means by which one may gather, classify, and organize useful knowledge, through harmonious alliance of two or more minds, out of which grows a Master Mind.

I have searched in vain through all the textbooks and essays available on the subject of the human mind, but found nowhere even the slightest reference to the principle here described as the Master Mind. The term first came to my attention through an interview with Andrew Carnegie, in the manner described in Lesson Two.

MIND CHEMISTRY

It is my belief that the mind is made up of the same universal energy as that which fills the universe. It is a fact as well known to the layman as to the scientist, that some minds clash the moment they come in contact with each other, while other minds show a natural affinity for each other. Between the two extremes of natural antagonism and natural affinity growing out of the meeting or contacting of minds there is a wide range of possibility for varying reactions of mind upon mind.

Some minds are so naturally adapted to each other that love at first sight is the inevitable outcome of the contact. Who has not known of such an experience? In other cases minds are so antagonistic that violent mutual dislike shows itself at first meeting. These results occur without a word being spoken, and without the slightest signs of any of the usual causes for love and hate acting as a stimulus.

It is quite probable that the mind is made up of energy, and when two minds come close enough to each other to form a contact, the mixing of the units of this mind stuff sets up a chemical reaction and starts vibrations which affect the two individuals pleasantly or unpleasantly.

The effect of the meeting of two minds is obvious to even the most casual observer. Every effect must have a cause! What could be more reasonable than to suspect that the cause of the change in mental attitude between two minds which have just come in close contact is none other than the disturbance of the electrons or units of each mind in the process of rearranging themselves in the new field created by the contact?

For the purpose of establishing this lesson upon a sound foundation we have gone a long way toward success by admitting that the meeting or coming in close contact of two minds sets up in each of those minds a certain noticeable effect or state of mind quite different from the one existing immediately prior to the contact. While it is desirable, it is not essential to know what is the cause of this reaction of mind upon mind. That the reaction takes place, in every instance, is a known fact which gives us a starting point from which we may show what is meant by the term Master Mind.

A Master Mind may be created through the bringing together or blending, in a spirit of perfect harmony, of two or more minds. Out of this harmonious blending the chemistry of the mind creates a third mind which may be appropriated and used by one or all of the individual minds. This Master Mind will remain available as long as the friendly, harmonious alliance between the individual minds exists. It will disintegrate and all evidence of its former existence will disappear the moment the friendly alliance is broken.

COMMENTARY

There is a strong parallel between what Hill here is saying about the interrelation of minds and the theories of the revolutionary philosopher/scientist/designer Buckminster Fuller. In the introduction to Synergetics, *Fuller writes, "[H]umanity has been deprived of comprehensive understanding. Specialization has bred feelings of isolation, futility, and confusion in individuals." Hill believed that the Master Mind draws its members out of their fields of specialization into a group the power of which is greater than its component parts.*

Macrocosmically, Fuller says that we must understand all elements and operations of the universe as interconnected. In Synergetics *303.00 he defines* Universe *as, "The comprehensive, historically synchronous, integral-aggregate system embracing all the separate integral-aggregate systems of all men's consciously apprehended and communicated (to self or others) nonsimultaneous, nonidentical, but always complementary and only partially overlapping, macro-micro, always-and-everywhere, omnitransforming, physical and metaphysical, weighable and unweighable event sequences. Universe is a dynamically synchronous scenario..."*

The Meeting of Minds

This principle of mind chemistry is the basis and cause for practically all the soul-mate and eternal triangle cases, so many of which unfortunately find their way into the divorce courts and meet with popular ridicule from ignorant and uneducated people who manufacture vulgarity and scandal out of one of the greatest of Nature's laws.

The entire civilized world knows that the first two or three years of association after marriage are often marked by much disagreement, of a more or less petty nature. These are the years of adjustment. If the marriage survives them it is more than apt to become a permanent alliance. These facts no experienced married person will deny. Again we see the effect without understanding the cause.

TO BELIEVE

IN THE HEROIC

MAKES HEROES.

—Disraeli

While there are other contributing causes, yet, in the main, lack of harmony during these early years of marriage is due to the slowness of the chemistry of the minds in blending harmoniously. Stated differently, the electrons or units of the energy called the mind are often neither extremely friendly nor antagonistic upon first contact; but, through constant association they gradually adapt themselves in harmony, except in rare cases where association has the opposite effect of leading, eventually, to open hostility between these units.

It is a well-known fact that after a man and a woman have lived together for ten to fifteen years they become practically indispensable to each other, even though there may not be the slightest evidence of the state of mind called love. Moreover, this association and relationship not only develops a natural affinity between the two minds sexually, but it actually causes the two people to take on a similar facial expression and to resemble each other closely in many other marked ways.

So marked is the effect of the chemistry of the human mind that any experienced public speaker may quickly interpret the manner in which his statements are accepted by his audience. Antagonism in the mind of but one person in an audience of one thousand may be readily detected by the speaker who has learned how to feel and register the effects of antagonism. Moreover, the public speaker can make these interpretations without observing or in any manner being influenced by the expression on the faces of those in his audience. On account of this fact an audience may cause a speaker to rise to great heights of oratory, or heckle him into failure, without making a sound or denoting a single expression of satisfaction or dissatisfaction through the features of the face.

All master salesmen know the moment the "psychological time for closing" has arrived; not by what the prospective buyer says, but from the effect of the chemistry of his mind as interpreted or felt by the salesman. Words often belie the intentions of those speaking them but a correct interpretation of the chemistry of the mind leaves no loophole for such a possibility. Every able salesman knows that the majority of buyers have the habit of affecting a negative attitude almost to the very climax of a sale.

Every able lawyer has developed a sixth sense whereby he is enabled to feel his way through the most artfully selected words of the clever witness who is lying and correctly interpret that which is in the witness's mind, through the chemistry of the mind. Many lawyers have developed this ability without knowing the real source of it; they possess the technique without the scientific understanding upon which it is based. Many salesmen have done the same thing.

One who is gifted in the art of correctly interpreting the chemistry of the minds of others may, figuratively speaking, walk in at the front door of the mansion of a given mind and leisurely explore the entire building, noting all its details, walking out again with a complete picture of the interior of the building, without the owner of the building so much as knowing that he has entertained a visitor. It will be observed, in Lesson Eleven on accurate thought that this principle may be put to a very practical use (having reference to the principle of the chemistry of the mind).

Enough has already been stated to introduce the principle of mind chemistry, and to prove, with the aid of your own everyday experiences and casual observations that the moment two minds come within close range of each other a noticeable mental change takes place in both, sometimes registering in the nature of antagonism and at other times registering in the nature of friendliness. Every mind has what might be termed an electric field. The nature of this field varies, depending upon the mood of the individual mind back of it and upon the nature of the chemistry of the mind creating the field.

It is my belief that the normal or natural condition of the chemistry of any individual mind is the result of his physical heredity plus the nature of thoughts which have dominated his or her mind. I mean that every mind is continuously changing to the extent that the individual's philosophy and general habits of thought change the chemistry of mind. This is my theory. That any individual may voluntarily change the chemistry of his or her mind so that it will attract or repel all with whom it comes in contact is a *known fact!* Stated in another manner, any person may assume a mental attitude which will attract and please others or repel and antagonize them, and this without the aid of words or facial expression or other form of bodily movement or demeanor.

Go back, now, to the definition of a Master Mind—a mind which grows out of the blending and coordination of two or more minds, *in a spirit of perfect harmony,* and you will catch the full significance of the word *harmony.* Two minds will not blend nor can they be coordinated unless the element of perfect harmony is present. That is the secret of success or failure of practically all business and social partnerships.

Every sales manager and every military commander and every leader in any other walk of life understands the necessity of an *esprit de corps*— a spirit of common understanding and cooperation—in the attainment of success. This mass spirit of harmony of purpose is obtained through discipline, voluntary or forced, of such a nature that the individual minds become blended into a Master Mind. That is, the chemistry of the individual minds is modified in such a manner that these minds blend and function as one.

The methods through which this blending process takes place are as numerous as the individuals engaged in the various forms of leadership. Every leader has a method of coordinating the minds of his or her followers. One will use force. Another uses persuasion. One will play upon the fear of penalties while another plays upon rewards. The aim will be to reduce the individual minds of a given group of people to the point that they may be blended into a mass mind. You will not have to search deeply into history of statesmanship, politics, business, or finance, to discover the technique employed by the leaders in these fields in the process of blending the minds of individuals into a mass mind.

IF YOU DO NOT BELIEVE

IN COOPERATION,

LOOK WHAT HAPPENS

TO A WAGON THAT

LOSES A WHEEL.

The really great leaders of the world, however, have been provided by Nature with mind chemistry favorable as a nucleus of attraction for other minds. Napoleon was a notable example of a man possessing the magnetic type of mind, which had a very decided tendency to attract all minds with which it came in contact. Soldiers followed Napoleon to certain death without flinching, because of the impelling or attracting nature of his personality, and that personality was nothing more nor less than the chemistry of his mind.

COMMENTARY

Hill is here creating his own definition and explanation of "charisma," which originally meant a kind of religious power or leadership that made certain individuals unusually magnetic. The subject fascinated religious and political historians, psychologists, and other social scientists for many years. For a century after his death, because of the power he apparently was able to exert on those around him, Bonaparte was a prime example of a charismatic leader. When Hill first wrote The Law of Success, *Napoleon Bonaparte held the same kind of interest for many people that Hitler holds today.*

The Making of the Master Mind

No group of minds can be blended into a Master Mind if one of the individuals of that group possesses an extremely negative mind. The negative and positive minds will not blend in the sense here described as a Master Mind. Lack of knowledge of this fact has brought many an otherwise able leader to defeat.

Any able leader who understands this principle of mind chemistry may temporarily blend the minds of individuals into a mass mind, but the composition will disintegrate almost the very moment the leader's presence is removed from the group. The most successful life insurance sales organizations and other sales forces meet once a week, or more often, for the purpose of ... *of what?*

For the purpose of merging the individual minds into a Master Mind which will, for a few days, serve as a stimulus to the individual minds!

It may be, and generally is, true that the leaders of these groups do not understand what actually takes place in these meetings. The routine of such meetings is usually given over to talks by the leader and other members of the group, and occasionally from someone outside of the group; meanwhile the minds of the individuals are contacting and recharging one another.

The brain of a human being may be compared to an electric battery in that it will become exhausted or run down, causing the owner of it to feel despondent, discouraged, and lacking in energy. Who is so fortunate as never to have had such a feeling? The human brain, when in this depleted condition, must be recharged, and the manner in which this is done is through contact with a more vital mind or minds.

COMMENTARY

A great deal of New Age thinking and the study of the practices of Asian philosophy and religion have created a number of ways unknown to Hill of "recharging the mind." Yoga, meditation, various forms of prayer, spinning, and other techniques all have their devotees. The latter part of the twentieth century also saw tremendous interest in what is often referred to as the personal-growth or human-potential movement. It has fostered countless bestselling books, audio tape courses, video programs, and every week thousands of people pay to attend seminars, lectures, and retreats to hear motivational speakers or spiritual leaders inspire them to be better at some aspect of their lives.

Some pundits have belittled the lasting effects of such techniques, referring to those who attend as seminar-junkies who need a new guru every week to get themselves pumped up. Hill would not have agreed with such a cynical view. He saw diminishing motivation as a perfectly logical aspect of human nature.

Sexuality and the Master Mind

The great leaders understand the necessity of this recharging process, and, moreover, they understand how to accomplish this result. *This knowledge is the main feature that distinguishes a leader from a follower!* Fortunate is the person who understands this principle sufficiently well to keep his or her brain vitalized or recharged by periodically connecting it with a more vital mind.

Sexual contact is one of the most effective of the stimuli through which a mind may be recharged, providing the contact is intelligently made, between man and woman who have genuine affection for each other. (Any other sort of sexual relationship is a devitalizer of the mind.) Any competent practitioner of psychotherapy can recharge a brain within a few minutes.

Before passing away from the brief reference made to sexual contact as a means of revitalizing a depleted mind it seems appropriate to call attention to the fact that all of the great leaders, in whatever walks of life they have arisen, have been and are people of highly sexed natures.

COMMENTARY

Hill's position on the relationship between sexuality and creativity is complex and changes several times throughout his life. While here recommending the bond between a man and a woman he seems not to feel impelled to recommend that leaders draw women into their Master Mind groups. In later works, notably Think and Grow Rich, *he alters his position to recommend sublimation of sexual energy.*

A factor in this may be that Hill seems to have perceived his audience to be entirely masculine. (Practically speaking, the business climate of the 1920s and 1930s did not encourage independent achievement by women.) In the original version of The Law of Success, *virtually all examples are of men, and references to human potentiality are always written with masculine examples. (He talks, for example, about what a man may or must do.)*

There is a growing tendency upon the part of the best-informed physicians and other health practitioners, to accept the theory that all diseases begin when the brain of the individual is in a depleted or devitalized state. Stated in another way, a person who has a perfectly vitalized brain is practically, if not entirely, immune from disease.

Health practitioners know that Nature, or the mind, cures disease in every instance where a cure is effected. Medicines, faith, laying on of hands, chiropractic, osteopathy, and all other forms of outside stimulant are nothing more than aids to Nature, or, to state it correctly, mere methods of setting the chemistry of the mind into motion to the end that it readjusts the cells and tissues of the body, revitalizes the brain, and otherwise causes the human machine to function normally.

The most conventional practitioner will admit the truth of this statement.

What, then, may be the possibilities of the future developments in the field of mind chemistry?

Through the principle of harmonious blending of minds, perfect health may be enjoyed. Through the aid of this same principle sufficient power may be developed to solve the problem of economic pressure which constantly presses upon every individual.

We may judge the future possibilities of mind chemistry by taking inventory of its past achievements, keeping in mind the fact that these achievements have been largely the result of accidental discovery and of chance groupings of minds.

COMMENTARY

In his references to health and the power of the mind, Napoleon Hill once again demonstrates not only insight, but also what can now be seen as foresight. From the 1960s through the end of the century, what is now commonly called the body-mind connection moved from the fringes of the New Age into the mainstream of American life.

Virtually every newspaper, television news program, and popular magazine regularly features stories on the crucial role the mind plays in helping the immune system to heal the body. Techniques to utilize the healing powers of the mind are now taught in most medical schools and are the basis of bestselling books by Dr. O. Carl Siminton, Louise Haye, Dr. Bernie Segal, Ken Dychtwald, Dr. Deepak Chopra, and Dr. Andrew Weil, to mention but a few of the more high-profile authors.

Mind Chemistry and Economic Power

Mind chemistry may be appropriately applied to the workaday affairs of the economic and commercial world.

Through the blending of two or more minds in a spirit of perfect harmony the principle of mind chemistry may be made to develop sufficient power to enable the individuals whose minds have been thus blended to perform seemingly superhuman feats. Power is the force with which humans achieve success in any undertaking. Power, in unlimited quantities, may be enjoyed by any group of people who possess the wisdom with which to submerge their own personalities and their own immediate individual interests, through the blending of their minds in a spirit of perfect harmony.

Observe, profitably, the frequency with which the word harmony appears throughout this chapter! There can be no development of a Master Mind where this element of perfect harmony does not exist. The units of one mind will not blend with the units of another mind until the two minds have been aroused and warmed, as it were, with a spirit of perfect harmony of purpose. The moment two minds begin to take divergent roads of interest the individual units of each mind separate, and the third element, the Master Mind that grew out of the friendly or harmonious alliance, will disintegrate.

COMMENTARY

Before reading the following comments on Ford, Edison, and Firestone, once again it is worth noting that Hill wrote this work before many of the great fortunes of America were made, and before many of the industries and businesses that play a role in contemporary life were even conceived. Hill was writing at a time when the possibility of an airline industry was barely born, and the entertainment industries including the great Hollywood studios, the music business, and the television networks were still awaiting the inventions that would make them possible. IBM and the aerospace industry didn't exist, and the computer revolution and the Internet were hardly imaginable.

As this revised edition is being readied for publication in 2001, it seems somewhat anachronistic to imagine three such powerful business leaders getting together to share ideas. Today, instead of Ford, Firestone, and Edison it would be a group such as Bill Gates, Jeff Bezos, and Michael Dell. As interesting as such a meeting would probably be, it's hard to imagine them meeting in perfect harmony, and if they did they might well be violating a half-dozen anti-trust laws.

Anti-trust violations not withstanding, there are more than enough modern examples of the Master Mind at work. What else would you term the coming together of Speilberg, Katzenberg, and Geffen to create DreamWorks? And who hasn't heard the classic example of Wozniak and Jobs huddled in a garage putting together the first Apple computer that launched the computer revolution?

Examples of Mind Chemistry in Action

We come, now, to the study of some well-known men who have accumulated great power (also great fortunes) through the application of mind chemistry.

Let us begin our study with three men who are known to be men of great achievement in their respective fields of economic, business, and professional endeavor. Their names are Henry Ford, Thomas A. Edison, and Harvey S. Firestone.

Of the three Henry Ford is, by far, the most powerful, if measured in economic and financial power. Mr. Ford is the most powerful man now living on earth. Many who have studied Mr. Ford believe him to be the most powerful man who ever lived.

As far as is known Ford is the only person now living, or who ever lived, with sufficient power to outwit the money trust of the United States. Ford gathers millions of dollars with as great ease as a child fills its bucket with sand when playing on the beach. It has been said, by those who were in position to know, that Ford, if he needed it, could send out the call for money and gather in a billion dollars and have it available for use within one week. No one who knows Ford's achievements doubts this. Those who know him well know that he could do it with no more effort than the average person expends in raising the money to pay a month's house rent. He could get this money, if he needed it, through the intelligent application of the principles on which this course is based.

While Mr. Ford's new automobile was in the process of perfection, in 1927, it is said that he received advance orders, with cash payments, for more than 375,000 cars. At an estimated price of $600 per car this would amount to $225,000,000 which he received before a single car was delivered. Such is the power of confidence in Ford's ability.

Thomas Edison, as everyone knows, is a philosopher, scientist, and inventor. He is, perhaps, the keenest Bible student on earth, a student of Nature's Bible, however, and not of the myriad manmade Bibles. Mr. Edison has such a keen insight that he has harnessed and combined, for the good of mankind, more of Nature's laws than any other person now living or who ever lived. It was he who brought together the point of a needle and a piece of revolving wax, in such a way that the vibration of the human voice may be recorded and reproduced through the early phonograph.

Edison first harnessed lightning and made it serve as a light for man's use, through the aid of the incandescent bulb.

COURAGE IS

THE STANDING ARMY

OF THE SOUL

WHICH KEEPS IT

FROM CONQUEST, PILLAGE

AND SLAVERY.

—Henry van Dyke

Edison gave the world the modern moving picture.

These are but a few of his outstanding achievements. The miracles that he performed (not by trickery, under the sham pretense of super-human power, but in the very midst of the bright light of science) tran-scend all of the so-called miracles described in the manmade books of fiction.

Harvey Firestone is the moving spirit in the great Firestone Tire in-dustry, in Akron, Ohio.

All three of these men began their careers, business and professional, without capital and with little formal education. All three men are now well educated. All three are wealthy. All three are powerful.

Now let us inquire into the source of their wealth and power. Thus far we have been dealing only with effect; the true philosopher wishes to understand the cause of a given effect.

It is a matter of general knowledge that Ford, Edison, and Firestone are close personal friends, and have been so for many years; that in for-mer years they were in the habit of going away to the woods once a year for a period of rest, meditation, and recuperation.

But it is not generally known—it may be doubted that these men know it themselves—that there exists between the three men a bond of harmony which has caused their minds to become blended into a Master Mind which is the real source of the power of each. This mass mind, growing out of the coordination of the individual minds of Ford, Edison, and Firestone, has enabled these men to tune in on forces (and sources of knowledge) with which most people are unfamiliar.

More than half this theory is known fact. For example, it is known that these men have great power and that they are wealthy. It is also known that they began without capital and with little schooling. And it is known that they form periodic mind contacts. It is known that they are harmonious and friendly. It is known that their achievements are too outstanding to be easily compared with those of others in their re-spective fields of activity.

These men work with natural laws well known to all economists and natural scientists. As yet chemistry of the mind is not sufficiently developed to be classed, by scientific men, in their catalogue of known laws.

A Master Mind may be created by any group of people who will coordinate their minds, in a spirit of perfect harmony. The group may consist of any number from two upward. Best results appear available from the blending of six or seven minds.

It has been suggested that Jesus Christ discovered how to make use of the principle of mind chemistry, and that His seemingly miraculous performances grew out of the power He developed through the blending of the minds of the twelve disciples. It has been pointed out that when one of the disciples (Judas Iscariot) broke faith, the Master Mind immediately disintegrated and Jesus met with supreme catastrophe.

COMMENTARY

An opposite example is Adolf Hitler, whose ability to hold the minds of his people in thrall allowed him to dominate Europe, terrify the world, and commit countless crimes against humanity. His immoral use of the Master Mind was defeated only by a greater Master Mind in which leaders like Franklin Roosevelt and Winston Churchill united their people in a valiant effort. It is interesting to note that in the United States, many people had opposed going to war against Hitler and his allies. President Roosevelt, however, applied many of the principles of the Law of Success to persuade the public of the necessity and rightness of his course. Truly great leaders have the ability to create harmony where it does not already exist. Roosevelt's Master Mind, like that of Jesus Christ, survived his death. Hitler's perished with him.

Not every Master Mind changes the course of history, but they can still offer important and valuable contributions. In a time when it was unusual for women to start up businesses, Mary Kay Ash invested her life savings in developing and marketing a line of cosmetics. To make her venture a success, she created a Master Mind with the women who sold her products. Because so many doors to success were closed to women in that time, she found that when she gave her sales reps an opportunity no one else offered, they responded by working hard for themselves and for her. She used a series of distinctive, highly visible rewards as incentives, most notably the famous pink Mary Kay Cadillacs. Today, more than 200,000 women worldwide sell Mary Kay cosmetics, part of a powerfully successful Master Mind.

When two or more people harmonize their minds and produce the effect known as a Master Mind, each person in the group becomes vested with the power to contact and gather knowledge through the subconscious minds of all the other members of the group. This power becomes immediately noticeable, having the effect of stimulating the mind to a higher rate of vibration and otherwise evidencing itself in the form of a more vivid imagination and the consciousness of what appears to be a sixth sense. It is through this sixth sense that new ideas will flash into the mind. These ideas take on the nature and form of the subject dominating the mind of the individual. If the entire group has met for the purpose of discussing a given subject, ideas concerning that subject will come pouring into the minds of all present, as if an outside influence were dictating them. The minds of those participating in the Master Mind become like magnets, attracting ideas and thoughts of the most highly organized and practical nature, from no one knows where!

The process of mind-blending here described as a Master Mind may be likened to the act of one who connects many electric batteries to a single transmission wire, thereby stepping up the power flowing over that line. Each battery added increases the power passing over that line by the amount of energy the battery carries. Just so in the case of blending individual minds into a Master Mind. Each mind, through the principle of mind chemistry, stimulates all the other minds in the group, until the mind energy thus becomes so great that it penetrates to and connects with the universal energy known as ether, which, in turn, touches every atom of the entire universe.

The modern radio apparatus substantiates, to a considerable extent, the theory here expounded. Powerful sending or broadcasting stations must be erected through which the vibration of sound is stepped up before it can be picked up by the much higher vibrating energy of the ether and carried in all directions. A Master Mind made up of many individual minds, so blended that they produce a strong vibrating energy, constitutes almost an exact counterpart of the radio broadcasting station.

Every public speaker has felt the influence of mind chemistry, for it is a well-known fact that as soon as the individual minds of an audience become en rapport (attuned to the rate of vibration of the mind of the speaker) with the speaker, there is a noticeable increase of enthusiasm in the speaker's mind, and he often rises to heights of oratory which surprise all, including himself.

The first five to ten minutes of the average speech are devoted to what is known as warming up. By this is meant the process through which the minds of the speaker and his audience are becoming blended in a spirit of *perfect harmony*.

Every speaker knows what happens when this state of perfect harmony fails to materialize upon part of his audience.

The seemingly supernatural phenomena occurring in spiritualistic meetings are the result of the reaction, upon one another, of the minds in the group. These phenomena seldom begin to manifest themselves in less than ten to twenty minutes after the group is formed, for the reason that this is about the time required for the minds in the group to become harmonized or blended.

Vibrations

The "messages" received by members of a spiritualistic group probably come from one of two sources, or from both:

• From the vast storehouse of the subconscious mind of some member of the group; or

• From the universal storehouse, in which I believe all thought vibration is preserved.

Neither any known natural law nor human reason supports the theory of communication with individuals who have died.

Any individual may explore the store of knowledge in another's mind through this principle of mind chemistry, and it seems reasonable to suppose that this power may be extended to include contact with whatever vibrations are available in the ether, if there are any.

Matter and energy (the two known elements of the universe) may be transformed but neither created nor destroyed. The theory that all the higher and more refined vibrations, such as those of thought, are preserved grows out of that fact. It is reasonable to suppose that all vibrations which have been stepped up sufficiently will go on forever. The lower vibrations probably live a natural life and die out.

All the so-called geniuses probably gained their reputations because, by mere chance or otherwise, they formed alliances with other minds which enabled them to step up their own mind vibrations and enabled to contact the vast Temple of Knowledge recorded and filed in the ether of the universe.

Inquiring further into the source of economic power, as manifested by the achievements of men in the field of business, let us study the case of the Chicago group known as the Big Six, consisting of William Wrigley, Jr., who owns the chewing gum business bearing his name, and whose individual income is said to be more than $15 million a year; John R. Thompson, who operates the chain of lunch rooms bearing his name; Mr. Lasker, who owns the Lord & Thomas Advertising Agency; Mr. McCullough, who owns the Parmalee Express Company, the largest transfer business in America; and Mr. Ritchie and Mr. Hertz, who own the Yellow Taxicab business. A reliable financial reporting company has estimated the yearly income of these six men at upward of $25 million, or an average of more than $4 million a year per man.

MEN CEASE TO INTEREST US

WHEN WE FIND THEIR LIMITATIONS.

THE ONLY SIN IS LIMITATION.

AS SOON AS YOU ONCE

COME UP TO A MAN'S LIMITATIONS,

IT IS ALL OVER WITH HIM.

—Emerson

Analysis of the entire group of six men discloses the fact that not one of them had any special educational advantages; that all began without capital or extensive credit; that their financial achievement has been due to their own individual plans, and not to any fortunate turn of the wheel of chance.

Many years ago these six men formed a friendly alliance, meeting at stated periods for the purpose of assisting one another with ideas and suggestions in their various lines of business.

With the exception of Hertz and Ritchie, none of the six men was in any manner associated in a legal partnership. These meetings were strictly for the purpose of cooperating on a give and take basis, assisting one another with ideas and suggestions, and occasionally endorsing notes and other securities to assist some member of the group who had met with an emergency.

It is said that each of the individuals belonging to this Big Six group is a millionaire many times over. As a rule there is nothing worthy of special comment on behalf of a man who does nothing more than accumulate a few million dollars. However, there is something connected with the financial success of this particular group of men that is well worth comment, study, analysis, and even emulation, and that something is the fact that they have learned how to coordinate their individual minds by blending them in a spirit of perfect harmony, thereby creating a Master Mind that unlocks, to each individual of the group, doors which are closed to most of the human race.

The United States Steel Corporation is one of the strongest and most powerful industrial organizations in the world. The idea out of which this great industrial giant grew was born in the mind of Elbert H. Gary, a more or less commonplace small-town lawyer who was born and reared near Chicago.

Mr. Gary surrounded himself with a group of men whose minds he successfully blended in a spirit of perfect harmony, thereby creating the Master Mind which is the moving spirit of the United States Steel Corporation.

Search where you will, wherever you find an outstanding success in business, finance, industry, or in any of the professions, you may be sure that back of the success is some individual who has applied the principle of mind chemistry, out of which a Master Mind has been created. These outstanding successes often appear to be the handiwork of but one person, but search closely and the other individuals whose minds have been coordinated with his own may be found. Remember that two or more persons may operate the principle of mind chemistry so as to create a Master Mind.

COMMENTARY

One of the most notable success stories of the computer age is the Intel corporation. As this edition is being readied for republication, Intel dominates the computer chip business worldwide, leading the quest to invent newer and faster chips. The most famous figure at Intel is Andrew Grove, the company's CEO, once an immigrant who supported himself waiting tables. Grove's keen skills as a manager, however, are only a part of the reason for Intel's success, for Grove is part of a Master Mind that includes Robert Noyce and Gordon Moore, the men whose technical knowledge and innovation helped drive the company forward. Each of these men is brilliant in his own right, but together they have made their company into the clear leader in its field—and one of the most consistently profitable businesses in the volatile high-tech industry.

Organized Knowledge

Power is organized knowledge, expressed through intelligent efforts. No effort can be said to be *organized* unless the individuals engaged in the effort coordinate their knowledge and energy in a spirit of perfect harmony. Lack of such harmonious coordination of effort is the main cause of practically every business failure.

I conducted an interesting experiment in collaboration with the students of a well-known college. Each student was requested to write an essay on "How and Why Henry Ford Became Wealthy."

Each student was required to describe, as a part of his or her essay, what was believed to be the nature of Ford's real assets, of what these assets consisted in detail.

The majority of the students gathered financial statements and inventories of the Ford assets and used these as the basis of their estimates of Ford's wealth.

The sources of Ford's wealth included cash in banks; raw and finished materials in stock, real estate, and buildings; good will, estimated at from 10 to 25 percent of the value of the material assets.

One student out of the entire group of several hundred answered as follows:

Henry Ford's assets consist, in the main, of two items, i.e., (1) Working capital and raw and finished materials; (2) The knowledge, gained from experience, of Henry Ford, himself, and the cooperation of a well trained organization which understands how to apply this knowledge to best advantage from the Ford viewpoint. It is impossible to estimate, with anything approximating correctness, the actual dollars and cents value of either of these two groups of assets, but it is my opinion that their relative values are:

The organized knowledge of the
Ford Organization   75 percent

The value of cash and physical assets of every
nature, including raw and finished materials   25 percent

Unquestionably the biggest asset that Henry Ford has is his own brain. Next to this would come the brains of his immediate circle of associates, for it has been through coordination of these that the physical assets that he controls were accumulated.

YOU CANNOT BECOME

A POWER IN YOUR COMMUNITY

NOR ACHIEVE ENDURING SUCCESS

IN ANY WORTHY UNDERTAKING

UNTIL YOU BECOME BIG ENOUGH

TO BLAME YOURSELF

FOR YOUR OWN MISTAKES

AND REVERSES.

Destroy every plant the Ford Motor Company owns: every piece of machinery, every atom of raw or finished material, every finished automobile, and every dollar on deposit in any bank, and Ford would still be the most powerful man, economically, on earth. The brains that have built the Ford business could duplicate it again in short order. Capital is always available, in unlimited quantities, to such brains as Ford's.

Ford is the most powerful man on earth (economically) because he has the keenest and most practical conception of the principle of *organized knowledge* of any man on earth.

Despite Ford's great power and financial success, it may be that he has blundered often in the application of the principles through which he accumulated this power. There is little doubt that Ford's methods of mind coordination have often been crude; they were bound to be so in the earlier days of his experience, before he gained the wisdom of application that would naturally go with maturity of years.

There can't be much doubt that Ford's application of the principle of mind chemistry was, at least at the start, the result of a chance alliance with other minds, particularly the mind of Edison. It is more than probable that Mr. Ford's remarkable insight into the laws of Nature was first begun as the result of his friendly alliance with his own wife long before he ever met either Mr. Edison or Mr. Firestone. Many a man who never knows the real source of his success is made by his wife, through application of the Master Mind principle. Mrs. Ford is a most remarkably intelligent woman, and I believe that it was her mind, blended with Mr. Ford's, which gave him his first real start toward power.

It may be mentioned, without in any way depriving Ford of any honor or glory, that in his earlier days he had to combat the powerful enemies of illiteracy and ignorance to a greater extent than did either Edison or Firestone, both of whom were gifted by natural heredity with a most fortunate aptitude for acquiring and applying knowledge. Ford had to hew this talent out of the rough, raw timbers of his hereditary estate.

Within an inconceivably short period of time Ford has mastered three of the most stubborn enemies of mankind and transformed them into assets constituting the very foundation of his success.

These enemies are: ignorance, illiteracy, and poverty!

Anyone who can stay the hand of these three savage forces, much less harness and use them to good account, is well worth close study by the less fortunate individuals.

This is an age of *industrial power* in which we are living! The source of all this *power* is *organized effort*. Not only has the management of industrial enterprises efficiently organized individual workers, but, in many instances, mergers of industry have been effected in such a manner and to the end that these combinations (as in the case of the United States Steel Corporation, for example) have accumulated practically unlimited power.

One may hardly glance at the news of a day's events without seeing a report of some business, industrial, or financial merger, bringing under one management enormous resources and thus creating great power.

One day it is a group of banks; another day it is a chain of railroads; the next day it is a combination of steel plants, all merging for the purpose of developing power through highly organized and coordinated effort.

Knowledge, general in nature and unorganized, is not *power*, it is only potential power—the raw material out of which real power may be developed. Any modern library contains an unorganized record of all the knowledge of value to which the present stage of civilization is heir, but this knowledge is not power because it is not organized.

Every form of energy and every species of animal or plant life, to survive, must be organized. The oversized animals whose remains have filled Nature's bone yard through extinction have left mute but certain evidence that non-organization means annihilation.

From the smallest particle of matter to the largest star in the universe, these and every material thing in between these two extremes offer proof positive that one of Nature's first laws is that of *organization*. Fortunate is the individual who recognizes the importance of this law and makes it his business to familiarize himself with the various ways in which the law may be applied to advantage.

The astute businessman has not only recognized the importance of the law of organized effort, but he has made this law the warp and the woof of his *power*.

Without any knowledge, whatsoever, of the principle of mind chemistry, or that such a principle exists, many influential persons have accumulated great power by merely organizing the knowledge they possessed. The majority of all who have discovered the principle of mind chemistry and developed that principle into a Master Mind have stumbled upon this knowledge by the merest of accident, often failing to recognize the real nature of their discovery or to understand the source of their power.

I am of the opinion that all living persons who at the present time are consciously making use of the principle of mind chemistry in developing power through the blending of minds may be counted on the fingers of the two hands, with, perhaps, several fingers left to spare.

If this estimate is even approximately true there is little danger that the field of mind chemistry will become overcrowded.

It is a well-known fact that one of the most difficult tasks anyone in business must perform is inducing associates to coordinate their efforts in a spirit of harmony. To induce continuous cooperation between a group of workers, in any undertaking, is next to impossible. Only the most efficient leaders can accomplish this highly desired objective, but once in a great while such a leader will rise above the horizon in the field of industry, business, or finance, and then the world hears of a Henry Ford, Thomas A. Edison, John D. Rockefeller, Sr., E. H. Harriman, or James J. Hill.

Power and success are practically synonymous terms!

One grows out of the other; therefore, any person who has the knowledge and the ability to develop power through the principle of harmonious coordination of effort between individual minds, or in any other manner, may be successful in any reasonable undertaking that is possible of successful termination.

Harmony

It must not be assumed that a Master Mind will immediately spring, mushroom fashion, out of every group of minds which make pretense of coordination in a spirit of *harmony!*

Harmony, in the real sense of meaning of the word, is as rare among groups of people as is genuine Christianity among those who proclaim themselves Christians.

Harmony is the nucleus around which the state of mind known as Master Mind must be developed. Without this element of harmony there can be no Master Mind, a truth which cannot be repeated too often.

Woodrow Wilson had in mind the development of a Master Mind to be composed of groups of minds representing the civilized nations of the world, in his proposal for establishing the League of Nations. Wilson's conception was the most far-reaching humanitarian idea ever created in the mind of man, because it dealt with a principle that embraces sufficient power to establish a real brotherhood of man on earth. The League of Nations, or some similar blending of international minds in a spirit of harmony, is sure to become a reality.

COMMENTARY

The League of Nations that Hill refers to was established in 1920, after the First World War, for the purpose of promoting world peace and cooperation. And though it was first proposed by President Woodrow Wilson, the United States never joined the organization which seriously impeded its effectiveness.

After the Second World War, The League of Nations was superceded by the creation of the United Nations of which America was one of the founding nations. Unfortunately the UN has not often lived up to Hill's conception of a Master Mind, which requires that the participants come together in perfect harmony.

The time when such unity of minds will take place will be measured largely by the time required for the great universities and non-sectarian institutions of learning to supplant ignorance and superstition with understanding and wisdom. This time is rapidly approaching.

COMMENTARY

Failure to develop a Master Mind can create enormous, embarrassing fiascoes. The Metropolitan Transit Authority of New York owned a valuable piece of property on Columbus Circle, one of the city's busiest intersections. The old Coliseum there had been made obsolete by a new Convention Center, so the Transit Authority decided to sell the land to a developer for a new building. Several companies bid, and a winner was selected. When the design for the building was unveiled, however, there was enormous public outcry, for the building was so large that its shadow would lie over vast stretches of Central Park.

So the developers paid for a new building design, but it, too, was greeted with public dismay, for it made only a token effort to address the many objections. Citizen groups circulated petitions and threatened lawsuits. Wealthy individuals who lived in the neighborhood protested just as loudly as people on the street, because all felt that the park was threatened. The Transit Authority, the developer, even the city government tried to make the building happen, but at every turn they were stymied by people who were outraged.

Finally, the developer gave up. Hundreds of millions of dollars had been spent on the project, the Transit Authority lost its sale, construction jobs were lost, and the Coliseum sat empty and unused for a decade. All this because the leaders of the project failed to create harmony among the people of the city.

NEVER, IN THE HISTORY

OF THE WORLD, HAS THERE BEEN

SUCH ABUNDANT OPPORTUNITY

AS THERE IS NOW FOR THE PERSON

WHO IS WILLING TO SERVE

BEFORE TRYING TO COLLECT.

The Psychology of the Revival Meeting

The old religious orgy known as the revival offers a favorable opportunity to study the principle of mind chemistry known as Master Mind.

It will be observed that music plays no small part in bringing about the harmony essential to the blending of a group of minds in a revival meeting. Without music the revival meeting would be a tame affair.

During revival services the leader of the meeting has no difficulty in creating harmony in the minds of his devotees, but it is a well-known fact that this state of harmony lasts no longer than the presence of the leader, after which the Master Mind he has temporarily created disintegrates.

By arousing the emotional nature of his followers, the revivalist has no difficulty, with the proper stagesetting music, in creating a Master Mind which becomes noticeable to all who come in contact with it. The very air becomes charged with a positive, pleasing influence that changes the entire chemistry of all minds present.

The revivalist calls this energy "the Spirit of the Lord."

Through experiments conducted with a group of scientific investigators and laymen (who were unaware of the nature of the experiment), I have created the same state of mind and the same positive atmosphere without calling it the Spirit of the Lord.

On many occasions I have witnessed the creation of the same positive atmosphere in a group of men and women engaged in the business of salesmanship, without calling it the Spirit of the Lord.

I once helped conduct a school of salesmanship for Harrison Parker, founder of the Cooperative Society, of Chicago, and, by the use of the principle of mind chemistry that revivalists call the Spirit of the Lord, so transformed the nature of a group of three thousand men and women (all of whom were without former sales experience) that they sold more than $10 million worth of securities in less than nine months and earned more than $1 million for themselves.

It was found that the average person who joined this school would reach the zenith of his or her selling power within one week, after which it was necessary to revitalize the individual's brain through a group sales meeting. These sales meetings were conducted on very much the same order as are the modern revival meetings, with much the same stage equipment, including music and high-powered speakers who exhorted the salespeople.

COMMENTARY

Not to belabor the obvious, but the style of presentation that Hill refers to in commenting on the similarity between revival meetings and his sales meetings can also be seen at almost any self-help or personal growth seminar.

Call it religion, psychology, mind chemistry, or anything you please (they are all based upon the same principle), but there is nothing more certain than the fact that wherever a group of minds are brought into contact, in a spirit of *perfect harmony*, each mind in the group becomes immediately supplemented and reinforced by a noticeable energy called a Master Mind.

For all this writer professes to know this uncharted energy may be the Spirit of the Lord, but it operates just as favorably when called by any other name. The human brain and nervous system constitute a piece of intricate machinery which but few, if any, understand. When controlled and properly directed this piece of machinery can be made to perform wonders of achievement and if not controlled it will perform wonders fantastic and phantomlike in nature, as may be seen by examining the inmates of any insane asylum.

The human brain has direct connection with a continuous influx of energy from which we derive our power to think. The brain receives this energy, mixes it with the energy created by the food taken into the body, and distributes it to every portion of the body, through the aid of the blood and the nervous system. It thus becomes what we call life.

Every normal human body possesses a first-class chemical laboratory and a stock of chemicals sufficient to carry on the business of breaking up, assimilating, and properly mixing and compounding the food we take into the body, preparatory to distributing it to wherever it is needed as a body builder.

Tests have been made, both with humans and animals, to prove that the energy known as the mind plays an important part in this chemical operation of compounding and transforming food into the required substances to build and keep the body in repair. It is known that worry, excitement, or fear will interfere with the digestive process, and in extreme cases stop this process altogether, resulting in illness or death. It is obvious, then, that the mind enters into the chemistry of food digestion and distribution.

It is believed by many eminent authorities, although it may never have been scientifically proved, that the energy known as mind or thought may become contaminated with negative or "unsociable" elements causing the whole nervous system to be thrown out of working order—digestion is interfered with and various diseases will manifest themselves. Financial difficulties and unrequited love affairs head the list of causes of such emotional disturbances.

A negative environment, such as that existing where some member of the family is constantly nagging, will interfere with the chemistry of the mind to the point that the individual loses ambition and gradually sinks into oblivion. It is because of this fact that the old saying that a man's wife may either make or break him is literally true. In a subsequent lesson a whole chapter on this subject is addressed to spouses.

Anyone knows that certain food combinations will, if taken into the stomach, result in indigestion, violent pain, and even death. Good health depends, in part at least, upon a food combination that harmonizes. But harmony of food combinations is not sufficient to insure good health; there must be harmony, also, between the elements of energy known as the mind.

———

A MAN IS HALF WHIPPED

THE MINUTE HE BEGINS

TO FEEL SORRY FOR HIMSELF,

OR TO SPIN AN ALIBI

WITH WHICH HE WOULD

EXPLAIN AWAY HIS DEFECTS.

———

Harmony

Harmony seems to be one of Nature's laws, without which there can be no such thing as organized energy, or life in any form whatsoever.

The health of the body as well as the mind is literally built around, out of, and upon the principle of harmony! The energy known as life begins to disintegrate and death approaches when the organs of the body stop working in harmony.

The moment harmony ceases at the source of any form of organized energy (power) the units of that energy are thrown into a chaotic state of disorder and the power is rendered neutral or passive.

Harmony is also the nucleus around which the principle of mind chemistry known as a Master Mind develops power. Destroy this harmony and you destroy the power that can grow out of the coordinated effort of a group of individual minds.

This truth has been stated, restated, and presented in every manner that I could conceive, with unending repetition; unless you grasp this principle and learn to apply it this lesson is useless.

Success in life, no matter what one may call success, is very largely a matter of adaptation to environment in such a manner that there is harmony between the individual and his environment. The palace of a king becomes as a hovel of a peasant if harmony does not abound within its walls. Conversely, the hut of a peasant may be made to yield more happiness than the mansion of the rich man, if harmony obtains in the former and not in the latter.

Without perfect harmony the science of astronomy would be as useless as the bones of a saint because the stars and planets would clash with one another, and all would be in a state of chaos and disorder.

Without the law of harmony an acorn might grow into a heterogeneous tree consisting of the wood of the oak, poplar, maple, and what not.

Without the law of harmony there can be no organization of knowledge, for what, may one ask, is organized knowledge except the harmony of facts and truths and natural laws?

The moment discord begins to creep in at the front door harmony edges out at the back door, so to speak, whether the application is made to a business partnership or the orderly movement of the planets of the heavens.

If you gather the impression that I am laying undue stress upon the importance of *harmony*, remember that lack of harmony is the first, and often the last and only, cause of failure!

There can be no poetry nor music nor oratory worthy of notice without the presence of harmony.

Good architecture is largely a matter of harmony. Without harmony a house is nothing but a mass of building material, more or less a monstrosity.

Sound business management plants the very sinews of its existence in harmony.

Every well-dressed man or woman is a living picture and a moving example of harmony.

With all these workaday illustrations of the important part which harmony plays in the affairs of the world—nay, in the operation of the entire universe—how could any intelligent person leave harmony out of his Definite Chief Aim in life? Could any definite aim in life omit harmony as the chief stone of its foundation?

KNOWLEDGE AND POWER

The human body is a complex organization of organs, glands, blood vessels, nerves, brain cells, muscles, etc. The mind that stimulates to action and coordinates the efforts of the component parts of the body is also a plurality of ever-varying and changing energies. From birth until death there is continuous struggle, often assuming the nature of open combat, between the forces of the mind. For example, the life-long struggle between the motivating forces and desires of the human mind, which takes place between the impulses of right and wrong, is well known to everyone.

Every human being possesses at least two distinct personalities, and as many as six distinct personalities have been discovered in one person. One of man's most delicate tasks is that of harmonizing these mind forces so that they may be organized and directed toward the orderly attainment of a given objective. Without this element of harmony no individual can become an accurate thinker.

It is no wonder that leaders in business and industrial enterprises, as well as those in politics and other fields of endeavor, find it so difficult to organize groups of people so they will function in the attainment of a given objective, without friction. Each individual human being possesses inner forces that are hard to harmonize, even when placed in the environment most favorable to harmony. If the chemistry of the individual's mind is such that the units of the mind cannot be easily harmonized, think how much more difficult it must be to harmonize a group of minds so they will function as one, in an orderly manner, through a Master Mind.

The leader who successfully develops and directs the energies of a Master Mind must possess tact, patience, persistence, self-confidence, intimate knowledge of mind chemistry, and the ability to adapt (in a state of perfect poise and harmony) to quickly changing circumstances, without showing the least sign of annoyance.

How many are there who can measure up to this requirement?

The successful leader must possess the ability to change the color of the mind, chameleonlike, to fit every circumstance that arises in connection with the object of leadership. Moreover, he or she must possess the ability to change from one mood to another without showing the slightest signs of anger or lack of self-control. The successful leader must understand the seventeen laws of success and be able to put into practice any combination of these seventeen laws whenever occasion demands.

Without this ability no leader can be powerful, and without power no leader can long endure.

The Meaning of Education

There has long been a general misconception of the meaning of the word *educate*. The dictionaries have not aided in the elimination of this misunderstanding, because they have defined the word *educate* as an act of imparting knowledge.

The word *educate* has its roots in the Latin word *educo*, which means to develop *from within*; to educe; to draw out; to grow through the law of *use*.

Nature hates idleness in all its forms. She gives continuous life only to those elements that are in use. Tie up an arm, or any other portion of the body, taking it out of use, and the idle part will soon atrophy and become lifeless. Reverse the order, give an arm more than normal use, such as that engaged in by the blacksmith who wields a heavy hammer all day long, and that arm (developed from within) grows strong.

Organized Knowledge in Action

Power grows out of *organized knowledge*, but, mind you, it grows out of it through application and use!

A person may become a walking encyclopedia of knowledge without possessing any power of value. This knowledge becomes power only to the extent that it is organized, classified, and put into action. Some of the best educated people the world has known possessed much less general knowledge than some who have been known as fools, the difference between the two being that the former put what knowledge they possessed into use while the latter made no such application.

An educated person is one who knows how to acquire everything needed in the attainment of the main purpose in life, without violating the rights of others. By that definition, many knowledgeable individuals come nowhere near qualifying as "educated." It might also be a great surprise to many who believe they suffer from lack of learning to know that they are well educated.

COMMENTARY

Henry Ford, as cited previously, is one example. Albert Einstein could barely eke out a living as a patent clerk until he began organizing his knowledge of physics. U.S. President Harry S. Truman had nothing more than a high school education. He laughed once that he was such a poor speller that when he wrote the word dictionary, "I had to look on the back to see how to spell the book itself." But all of these men commanded power in different ways.

The Uses of Learning

The successful lawyer is not necessarily the one who memorizes the greatest number of principles of law. On the contrary, the successful lawyer is the one who knows where to find a principle of law, plus a variety of opinions supporting that principle which fit the immediate needs of a given case.

In other words, the successful lawyer is the one who knows where to find the law he or she wants when needed.

This principle applies, with equal force, to the affairs of industry and business.

Henry Ford had but little elementary schooling, yet he is one of the best educated men in the world because he has acquired the ability to combine natural and economic laws, to say nothing of the minds of men, that he has the power to get anything of a material nature he wants.

During the First World War, Mr. Ford brought suit against the *Chicago Tribune*, charging that newspaper with libelous publication of statements concerning him, one of which was the statement that Ford was an "ignoramus," an ignorant pacifist, etc.

When the suit came up for trial the attorneys for the *Tribune* undertook to prove, through Ford himself, that their statement was true; that he was ignorant, and with this object in view they catechized and cross-examined him on all manner of subjects.

SEEK THE COUNSEL OF MEN

WHO WILL TELL YOU

THE TRUTH ABOUT YOURSELF,

EVEN IF IT HURTS YOU TO HEAR IT.

MERE COMMENDATION

WILL NOT BRING

THE IMPROVEMENT YOU NEED.

One question they asked was:

"How many soldiers did the British send over to subdue the rebellion in the Colonies in 1776?"

With a dry grin on his face Ford nonchalantly replied:

"I do not know just how many, but I have heard that it was a lot more than ever went back."

Loud laughter [erupted] from court, jury, courtroom spectators, and even from the frustrated lawyer who had asked the question.

This line of interrogation was continued for an hour or more, Ford keeping perfectly calm the meanwhile. Finally, however, he had permitted the smart alec lawyers to play with him until he was tired of it, and in reply to a question which was particularly obnoxious and insulting, Ford straightened himself up, pointed his finger at the questioning lawyer, and replied: "If I should really wish to answer the foolish question you have just asked, or any of the others you have been asking, let me remind you that I have a row of electric push buttons hanging over my desk and by placing my finger on the right button I could call in men who could give me the correct answer to all the questions you have asked and to many that you have not the intelligence either to ask or answer. Now, will you kindly tell me why I should bother about filling my mind with a lot of useless details in order to answer every fool question that anyone may ask, when I have able men all about me who can supply me with all the facts I want when I call for them?"

This answer is quoted from memory but it substantially relates Ford's answer.

There was silence in the courtroom. The questioning attorney's jaw dropped down, his eyes opened wide; the judge leaned forward from the bench and stared at Ford; many of the jury awoke and looked around as if they had heard an explosion (which they actually had).

A prominent clergyman who was present in the courtroom at the time said, later, that the scene reminded him of that which must have existed when Jesus Christ was on trial before Pontius Pilate, just after He had given His famous reply to Pilate's question, "Are you a king?"

In the vernacular of the day, Ford's reply knocked the questioner cold.

Up to the time of that reply the lawyer had been enjoying considerable fun at what he believed to be Ford's expense, by adroitly displaying his general knowledge and comparing it with what he inferred to be Ford's ignorance as to many events and subjects.

That answer spoiled the lawyer's fun!

It also proved once more (to all who had the intelligence to accept the proof) that true education means mind development, not merely the gathering and classifying of knowledge.

Ford could not, in all probability, have named the capitals of all the states of the United States, but he could have, and in fact had, gathered the "capital" with which to turn many wheels within every state in the Union.

Education—let us not forget this—consists of the power with which to get everything one needs when he needs it, without violating the rights of others. Ford comes well within that definition as the foregoing incident shows.

COMMENTARY

As the example of Henry Ford demonstrates, power is organized knowledge, expressed through intelligent efforts. Let us consider how a Master Mind facilitates the exercise of power. The current era has been called the Information Age, due in large part to the ease with which information is transferred through computers and modems, at speeds and in such volume that were unthinkable even a generation ago.

But information is not organized knowledge. In fact, one of the chief complaints of many people is that they have far more information at their disposal than they know what to do with. A few minutes surfing the Internet in search of the answer to a particular question can produce a deluge of conflicting, ambiguous information *that does nothing to increase one's* knowledge. *Thousands of facts may have been gathered, but an* understanding *of those facts, including which are significant and which are not, is necessary before they can be considered knowledge. Even such knowledge is not power; it is only potential power—the material out of which real power may be developed.*

The key to unlocking all this potential power is properly organized effort. Suppose you had collected the name and address of every CEO of a Fortune 500 company. Having this information represents a potential power—the ability to contact these men and women. Such power might or might not be useful to you. If you were attempting to sell a small starter home in need of much repair, you would be targeting a very unlikely group of buyers. If, on the other hand, you were selling a luxurious estate with state-of-the-art security and communications capability, this group of people would likely be more interested. Clearly, the knowledge you acquire must be suited to your task.

If you were indeed selling such an estate and you never attempted to contact these CEOs, however, you would not be exercising the potential power of your knowledge, simply because you made no effort. If you sent each of them a box of chocolates and some balloons with a handwritten note about your property, you would make an effort, but it would not be appropriate.

However, if you printed a handsome brochure featuring photographs of the estate and outlining all its unique qualities, you would be applying your knowledge much more usefully, giving you the power to attract the attention of your potential buyers.

So far, the selling of this estate has involved at least three separate tasks. First, the collection of the names of potential buyers; second, the creation of an appropriate selling tool; and third, its distribution to your potential buyers. Supposing you interested some of these people, you would also need someone to show the property and eventually to negotiate the terms of the deal. This means at least five different tasks, all requiring different kinds of knowledge. You could work to educate yourself for each of these jobs, or you could create a Master Mind.

You could begin enlisting a direct mail specialist to collect the list of names; that person could also contribute ideas for the brochure, which would be designed by a graphic artist familiar with all the necessary steps for production. You would handle showing the estate and selling it to your prospective buyers, and the fine points of the deal could be hammered out by an attorney. You would all be united behind a common purpose, dedicating your special skills to the task of making the sale. But who would have truly been responsible for making the sale happen? You, for it was you who assembled the team that got the job done.

The Uses of Learning

There are many learned people who could easily entangle Ford, theoretically, with a maze of questions none of which he, personally, could answer. But Ford could turn right around and wage a battle in industry or finance that would exterminate those same men, with all of their knowledge and all of their wisdom.

Ford could not go into his chemical laboratory and separate water into its component atoms of hydrogen and oxygen and then recombine these atoms in their former order, but he knows how to surround himself with chemists who can do this for him if he wants it done.

The person who can intelligently use the knowledge possessed by another is as much or more a person of education as the one who merely has the knowledge but does not know what to do with it.

The president of a well-known college inherited a large tract of very poor land. This land had no timber of commercial value, no minerals or other valuable appurtenances; therefore it was nothing but a source of expense to him, for he had to pay taxes on it. The state built a highway through the land. An "uneducated" man who was driving his automobile over this road observed that this poor land was on top of a mountain that commanded a wonderful view for many miles in all directions. He (the ignorant one) also observed that the land was covered with a growth of small pines and other saplings.

He bought fifty acres of the land for $10 an acre. Near the public highway he built a unique log house to which he attached a large dining room. Near the house he put in a gasoline filling station. He built a dozen single-room log houses along the road; these he rented out to tourists at $3 a night, each. The dining room, gasoline filling station, and log houses brought him a net income of $15,000 the first year. The next year he extended his plan by adding fifty more log houses, of three rooms each, which he now rents out as summer country homes to people in a nearby city, at a rental of $150 each for the season.

The building material cost him nothing, for it grew on his land in abundance (that same land which the college president believed to be worthless).

Moreover, the unique and unusual appearance of the log bungalows served as an advertisement of the plan, whereas many would have considered it a real calamity had they been compelled to build out of such crude materials.

Less than five miles from the location of these log houses this same man purchased an old worked-out farm of 150 acres, for $25 an acre, a price which the seller believed to be extremely high.

By building a dam, one hundred feet in length, the purchaser of this old farm turned a stream of water into a lake that covered fifteen acres of the land, stocked the lake with fish, then sold the farm off in building lots to people who wanted summering places around the lake. The total profit realized from this simple transaction was more than $25,000, and the time required for its consummation was one summer.

Yet this man of vision and imagination was not educated in the orthodox meaning of that term.

Let us keep in mind the fact that it is through these simple illustrations of the use of organized knowledge that one may become educated and powerful.

In speaking of the transaction here related, the college president who sold the fifty acres of "worthless" land for $500 said:

"Just think of it! That man, whom most of us might call ignorant, mixed his ignorance with fifty acres of worthless land and made the combination yield more yearly than I earn from five years of application of so-called education."

———————

There is an opportunity, if not scores of them, in every state in America, to make use of the idea here described. From now on make it your business to study the lay of all land you see that is similar to that described in this lesson, and you may find a suitable place for developing a similar money-making enterprise.

The automobile has caused a great system of public highways to be built throughout the United States. On practically every one of these highways there is a suitable spot for a "cabin city" for tourists which can be turned into a regular money-making mint by the person with the imagination and self-confidence to do it.

COMMENTARY

If you think that Hill's example of starting what we now know as a motel is out of date and no longer applicable, you are not seeing the ideas for the words.

As this edition is being edited, Hill's advice is almost seventy-five years old, yet one of the most exciting new business ventures of this era might well have been inspired by that "out of date" story. Jeff Bezos did exactly what Hill suggested. He looked for a highway on which to set up a business. When he found the right place he opened a bookstore. The highway that Bezos found was the information highway, and the bookstore was Amazon.com.

Sometimes the innovation requires specialized education or technical expertise, but just as often the business itself is not especially new, the innovation is in finding the right highway.

Lora Brody is another example of someone whose inspiration made her greater than the so-called experts. The author of several cookbooks, she noticed that many people were buying and enjoying the bread machines that have lately become so popular. But she also noticed that they were not fully satisfied with the bread they were making. Her first right move was to write a new cookbook for bread machines, which was an instant success. Then she took her good idea even further.

Huge corporations were manufacturing these machines. Other huge corporations were making mixes to use in them. But Brody alone realized that these appliances were different enough from traditional techniques that the old methods weren't enough. What bread machine bakers needed were additives, simple natural ingredients that professional bakeries used all the time. So she created a line of dough enhancers that could be added to any bread machine recipe, creating a better, more tasty loaf.

Soon her "Bread Machine Magic" was in grocery stores and cooks' catalogs around the country, making home bakers happier and Brody a wealthy and popular entrepreneur. The experts who had been involved in creating these machines, and the flour companies that thought to profit from their popularity, had looked right past a tremendous opportunity that one woman who organized her knowledge profited from.

In the mid-1970s, computers were used by big businesses. They were giant, complicated machines too expensive for anyone else to afford, or such was the conventional wisdom at companies like IBM. Steve Jobs and Steven Wozniak thought differently. In a garage in California, they built a small computer that could fit on a desktop. The company they founded was called Apple. The Apple computer created a revolution in the computer industry—and made multimillionaires of Jobs and Wozniak, because they organized their knowledge in a way that no one had before.

Ray Krok saw that people wanted fast food, and he created McDonalds. Frederick W. Smith saw that people wanted safe reliable delivery and created Federal Express. Bill Bowerman saw people jogging and created Nike to make special shoes for the new fad.

There are similar opportunities everywhere, in every walk of life, in every area of human endeavor, to achieve success. This course can reveal new opportunities and strategies for personal success. What it cannot do is give you the benefit of real education, of creating an understanding based on your own efforts. You must resolve to take the ideas that you absorb here and apply them in all your efforts.

As this course proceeds, you will learn more about the Master Mind, as well as all the other significant principles you must apply. You will begin to see how they all fit together into a harmonious whole, a manner of acting and thinking that takes best advantage of the way the world operates. But only through applying each of these principles will you truly understand how to integrate them.

Remember: your own actions will educate you in the Law of Success.

There are opportunities to make money all around you. This course was designed to help you see these opportunities and to inform you how to make the most of them after you discover them.

WHO CAN PROFIT MOST BY THE
LAW OF SUCCESS PHILOSOPHY?

Transportation Officials who want a better spirit of cooperation between their employees and the public they serve.

Salaried People who wish to increase their earning power and market their services to better advantage.

Salespeople who wish to become masters in their chosen field. The Law of Success philosophy covers every known law of selling and includes many features not included in any other course.

Industrial Plant Managers who understand the value of greater harmony among their employees.

Employees who wish to establish records of efficiency that will lead to more responsible positions, with greater pay.

Merchants who wish to extend their business by adding new customers. The Law of Success philosophy will help any merchant increase business by teaching how to make a walking advertisement of every customer who comes into the store.

Sales Agents or Managers who wish to increase the selling power of their sales force. A large part of the Law of Success course was developed from the life work and experience of the greatest automobile salesman, and it is therefore of unusual help to the sales manager who is directing the efforts of a sales force.

Life Insurance Agents who wish to add new policyholders and increase the insurance on present policyholders. One life insurance salesman, in Ohio, sold a $50,000 policy to one of the officials of the Central Steel Company, as the result of but one reading of the lesson on "Profiting by Failures." This same salesman has become one of the star men of the New York Life Insurance Company's staff, as the result of his training in the seventeen laws of success.

School Teachers who wish to advance to the top in their present occupation, or who are looking for an opportunity to enter the field of business as a life work.

Students, both college and high school, who are undecided as to what field of endeavor they wish to enter as a life work. The Law of Success course covers a complete personal analysis service that helps the student of the philosophy to determine the work for which he or she is best fitted.

Bankers who wish to extend their business through better and more courteous methods of serving their clients.

Mid-level Managers who are ambitious to prepare themselves for executive positions in the field of banking or in some commercial or industrial field.

Physicians and Dentists who wish to extend their practice without violating the ethics of their profession by direct advertising. A prominent physician has said that the Law of Success course is worth $1,000 to any professional man or woman whose professional ethics prevent direct advertising.

WHO SAID IT COULD NOT BE DONE?

AND WHAT GREAT VICTORIES

HAS HE TO HIS CREDIT

WHICH QUALIFY HIM

TO JUDGE OTHERS ACCURATELY?

Entrepreneurs and Promoters who wish to develop new and heretofore unworked combinations in business or industry.

The principle described in this introductory lesson is said to have made a small fortune for a man who used it as the basis of a real estate promotion.

Real Estate Agents who wish new methods for promoting sales. This introductory lesson contains a description of an entirely new real-estate promotion plan which is sure to make fortunes for many who will put it to use. This plan may be put into operation in practically every state. Moreover, it may be employed by agents who never promoted an enterprise.

Farmers who wish to discover new methods of marketing their products so as to give them greater net returns, and those who own lands suitable for subdivision promotion under the plan referred to at the end of this introductory lesson. Many farmers have "gold mines" in the land they own which is not suitable for cultivation, which could be used for recreation and resort purposes, on a highly profitable basis.

Entry-level Service Workers who are looking for a practical plan to promote themselves into higher and better paying positions. The Law of Success course is said to be the best course ever written on the subject of marketing personal services.

Printers who want a larger volume of business and more efficient production as the result of better cooperation among their own employees.

Laborers who have the ambition to advance into more responsible positions, in work that has greater responsibilities and consequently offers more pay.

Lawyers who wish to extend their clientele through dignified, ethical methods which will bring them to the attention, in a favorable way, of a greater number of people who need legal services.

Business Executives who wish to expand their present business, or who wish to handle their present volume with less expense, as the result of greater cooperation among their employees.

Service Industry Owners who wish to extend their business by teaching their drivers how to serve more courteously and efficiently.

Life Insurance General Agents who wish bigger and more efficient sales organizations.

Chain Store Managers who want a greater volume of business as the result of more efficient individual sales efforts.

Married People who are unhappy, and therefore unsuccessful, because of lack of harmony and cooperation in the home.

To all described in the foregoing classification the Law of Success philosophy offers both *definite* and *speedy* aid.

SUMMARY, THE MASTER MIND

The main purpose of this lesson is to state some of the principles upon which the course is founded. These principles are more accurately described, and the student is taught in a very definite manner how to apply them, in the individual lessons of the course.

All new ideas, and especially those of an abstract nature, find lodgment in the human mind only after much repetition, a well-known truth that accounts for the restatement, in this summary, of the principle known as the Master Mind.

A Master Mind may be developed by a friendly alliance, in a spirit of harmony of purpose, between two or more minds.

This is an appropriate place at which to explain that out of every alliance of minds, whether in a spirit of harmony or not, there is developed another mind which affects all participating in the alliance. No two or more minds ever met without creating, out of the contact, another mind, but this creation is not always a Master Mind.

There may be, and altogether too often there is, developed out of the meeting of two or more minds a negative power which is just the opposite of a Master Mind.

There are certain minds which, as has been stated throughout this lesson, cannot be made to blend in a spirit of harmony. This principle has its analogy in chemistry.

For example, the chemical formula H_2O (meaning the combining of two atoms of hydrogen with one atom of oxygen) changes these two elements into water. One atom of hydrogen and one atom of oxygen will not produce water; moreover, they cannot be made to associate themselves in harmony!

There are many known elements which, when combined, are immediately transformed from harmless into deadly poisonous substances. Stated differently, many well-known poisonous elements are neutralized and rendered harmless when combined with certain other elements.

Just as the combining of certain elements changes their entire nature, the combining of certain minds changes the nature of those minds, producing either a certain degree of what has been called a Master Mind or its opposite, which is highly destructive.

Some minds will not be harmonized and cannot be blended into a Master Mind, a fact that all leaders will do well to remember. It is the leader's responsibility to group his subordinates so that those who have been placed at the most strategic points in his organization are individuals whose minds can and will be blended in a spirit of friendliness and harmony.

Ability to bring people together is the chief outstanding quality of leadership. In Lesson Two of this course you will discover that this ability was the main source of both the power and fortune accumulated by the late Andrew Carnegie.

AN AIM IN LIFE

IS THE ONLY FORTUNE

WORTH FINDING;

AND IT IS NOT TO BE FOUND

IN FOREIGN LANDS,

BUT IN THE HEART ITSELF.

—Robert Louis Stevenson

Knowing nothing whatsoever of the technical end of the steel business, Carnegie so combined and grouped the people of which his Master Mind was composed that he built the most successful steel industry known to the world during his lifetime.

Henry Ford's gigantic success may be traced to the successful application of this selfsame principle. With all the self-reliance a man could have, Ford, nevertheless, did not depend upon himself for the knowledge necessary in the successful development of his industries.

Like Carnegie, he surrounded himself with people who supplied the knowledge which he, himself, did not and could not possess.

Moreover, Ford picked men who could and did harmonize in group effort.

The most effective alliances, which have resulted in the creation of the principle known as the Master Mind, have been those developed out of the blending of the minds of men and women. The reason for this is the fact that the minds of male and female will more readily blend in harmony than will the minds of only one gender. Also, the added stimulus of sexual contact often enters into the development of a Master Mind between a man and a woman.

The road to success may be, and generally is, obstructed by many influences that must be removed before the goal can be reached. One of the most detrimental of these obstacles is that of unfortunate alliance with minds which do not harmonize. In such cases the alliance must be broken or the end is sure to be defeat and failure.

Those who master the six basic fears, one of which is the fear of criticism, will have no hesitancy in taking what may seem to the more convention-bound type of mind to be drastic action when they find themselves circumscribed and bound down by antagonistic alliances, no matter of what nature or with whom they may be.

It is a million times better to meet and face criticism than to be dragged down to failure and oblivion on account of alliances which are not harmonious, whether the alliances be of a business or social nature.

While it is true that some minds will not blend in a spirit of harmony, and cannot be forced or induced to do so because of the chemical nature of the individuals' brains, do not be too ready to charge the other party to your alliance with all the responsibility of lack of harmony—remember, the trouble *may be with your own brain!*

Remember, also, that a mind that cannot and will not harmonize with one person or persons may harmonize perfectly with other types of minds. Discovery of this truth has resulted in radical changes in methods of hiring. It is no longer customary to discharge an employee who does not fit in the position for which he or she was originally hired. The discriminating leader endeavors to place such a person in some other position, where, it has been proved more than once, such individuals may become valuable.

You should be sure that the principle described as the Master Mind is thoroughly understood before proceeding with the remaining lessons of the course. The reason for this is the fact that practically the entire course is closely associated with this law of mind operation.

If you are not sure that you understand this law, analyze the record of anyone who has accumulated a great fortune, and you will find that they have, either consciously or unconsciously, employed the Master Mind principle.

You cannot spend too much time in serious thought and contemplation in connection with the Law of the Master Mind, for the reason that when you have mastered this law and have learned how to apply it new worlds of opportunity will open to you.

Any sales organization may make effective use of the Law of the Master Mind by grouping the sales force in groups of two or more people who will ally themselves in a spirit of friendly cooperation and apply this law as suggested in this lesson.

An agent for a well-known make of automobile, who employs a sales force of twelve, has grouped the organization in six groups of two each, with the object of applying the Law of the Master Mind, with the result that all the salespeople have established new high sales records.

This same organization has created what it calls the "One-A-Week Club," meaning that each person belonging to the club has averaged the sale of one car a week since the club was organized.

The results of this effort have been surprising to all! Each member of the club was provided with a list of one hundred prospective purchasers of automobiles. Each salesperson sends one post card a week to each of his one hundred prospective purchasers, and makes personal calls on at least ten of these each day.

Each card is confined to the description of but one advantage of the automobile and asks for a personal interview.

Interviews have increased rapidly, as have, also, sales!

The agent who employs the sales force has offered an extra cash bonus to anyone who earns the right to membership in the One-A-Week Club by averaging one car a week.

The plan has injected new vitality into the entire organization. Moreover, the results of the plan are showing in the weekly sales record. A similar plan could be adopted very effectively by life insurance agencies. Any enterprising general agent might easily double or even triple the volume of business through the use of this plan.

Practically no changes whatsoever would need to be made in the method of use of the plan. The club might be called the Policy-A-Week Club, meaning that each member pledges to sell at least one policy, of an agreed minimum amount, each week.

The student of this course who has mastered the second lesson, and understands how to apply the fundamentals of that lesson (a Definite Chief Aim) will be able to make much more effective use of the plan here described.

It is not suggested or intended that anyone undertake to apply the principles of this lesson, which is merely an introductory lesson, until he or she has mastered at least the next five lessons of the Law of Success course.

The automobile sales organization referred to in this summary meets at luncheon once a week. One hour and a half are devoted to

IF YOU CANNOT

DO GREAT THINGS YOURSELF,

REMEMBER THAT YOU MAY

DO SMALL THINGS

IN A GREAT WAY.

luncheon and to the discussion of ways and means of applying the principles of this course. This gives each individual member an opportunity to profit by the ideas of all the other members of the organization. Two tables are set for the luncheon.

At one table all who have earned the right to membership in the One-A-Week Club are seated. At the other table, which is serviced with tinware instead of china, are those who did not earn the right to membership in the Club are seated. These, needless to say, become the object of considerable good-natured chiding from the more fortunate members seated at the other table.

It is possible to make an almost endless variety of adaptations of this plan.

The justification for its use is that it pays!

It pays not only the leader or manager of the organization, but every member of the sales force as well.

This plan has been briefly described for the purpose of showing you how to make practical application of the principles outlined in this course.

The final acid test of any theory or rule or principle is that it will *actually work!* The Law of the Master Mind has been proved sound because it *works.*

If you understand this law you are now ready to proceed with Lesson Two, in which you will be further and much more deeply initiated in the application of the principles described in this introductory lesson.

—— Lesson Two ——

Your Definite Chief Aim

THE BEST ROSE BUSH,

AFTER ALL, IS NOT

THAT WHICH HAS

THE FEWEST THORNS,

BUT THAT WHICH BEARS

THE FINEST ROSES.

—Henry van Dyke

Lesson Two

YOUR DEFINITE CHIEF AIM

"You Can Do It If You Believe You Can!"

YOU ARE AT THE BEGINNING OF A COURSE OF philosophy which, for the first time in the history of the world, has been organized from the known factors which have been used and must always be used by successful people.

Literary style has been completely subordinated for the sake of stating the principles and laws included in this course in such a manner that they may be quickly and easily assimilated by people in every walk of life.

Some of the principles described in the course are familiar to all who will read the course. Others are here stated for the first time. It should be kept in mind, from the first lesson to the last, that the value of the philosophy lies entirely in the thought stimuli it will produce in the mind of the reader, and not merely in the lessons themselves.

Stated in another way, this course is intended as a mind stimulant that will cause you to organize and direct to a *definite* end the forces of your mind, thus harnessing the stupendous power which most people waste in purposeless thought.

Singleness of purpose is essential for success, no matter what may be one's idea of the definition of success. Yet singleness of purpose is a quality which may, and generally does, call for thought on many allied subjects.

I traveled a long distance to watch Jack Dempsey train for an on-coming battle. It was observed that he did not rely entirely upon one form of exercise, but resorted to many forms. The punching bag helped him develop one set of muscles and also trained his eye to be quick. The dumb-bells trained still another set of muscles. Running developed the muscles of his legs and hips. A well-balanced food ration supplied the materials needed for building muscle without fat. Proper sleep, relaxation, and rest habits provided still other qualities that he must have in order to win.

You should be engaged in the business of training for success in the battle of life. To win there are many factors which must have attention. A well-organized, alert, and energetic mind is produced by various and sundry stimuli, all of which are plainly described in these lessons.

It should be remembered, however, that the mind requires, for its de-velopment, a variety of exercise, just as the physical body, to be properly developed, calls for many forms of systematic exercise.

Horses are trained to certain gaits by trainers who jump them over hurdles to help them develop the desired steps, through habit and rep-etition. The human mind must be trained in a similar manner, by a va-riety of thought inspiring stimuli.

You will observe, before you have gone very far into this philosophy, that the reading of these lessons will induce a flow of thoughts covering a wide range of subjects. For this reason you should read the course with a notebook and pencil at hand, and follow the practice of recording these thoughts or ideas as they come into the mind.

By following this suggestion you will have a collection of ideas, by the time the course has been read two or three times, sufficient to transform your entire life plan.

By following this practice it will be noticed, very soon, that the mind has become like a magnet in that it will attract useful ideas right out of the thin air, to use the words of a noted scientist who has experimented with this principle for a great number of years.

COMMENTARY

In the time since Hill wrote these words, considerable research has been done on creativity, intuition, and various thinking styles and techniques. In almost all cases, books written on these subjects tend to support Hill's theory that the act of writing down what you think or dream prompts the human mind to make leaps of insight and spontaneously create original ideas. This in turn has prompted a whole subset of books about what is now termed journaling.

If you wish to explore the possibilities further you will find the following books of interest: The Intuitive Edge by Phillip Goldberg, The Right Brain Experience by Marilee Zdenak, Creative Dreaming by Patricia Garfield, Writing the Natural Way by Gabriel Ricco. Books on methods of thinking include numerous works by Tony Buzan, and an extensive collection of influential bestsellers written by Edward de Bono. Books on journaling include Writing Down the Bones by Natalie Goldberg, At a Journal Workshop by Ira Progoff, and The Artist's Way by Julia Cameron.

You will do yourself a great injustice if you undertake this course with even a remote feeling that you do not stand in need of more knowledge than you now possess. In truth, no human knows enough about any worthwhile subject to entitle him to feel that he has the last word on that subject.

In the long, hard task of trying to wipe out some of my own ignorance and make way for some of the useful truths of life, I have often seen, in my imagination, the Great Marker who stands at the gateway entrance of life and writes "Poor Fool" on the brow of those who believe they are wise, and "Poor Sinner" on the brow of those who believe they are saints.

Which, translated into workaday language, means that none of us know very much, and by the very nature of our being can never know as much as we need to know in order to live sanely and enjoy life while we live.

Humility is a forerunner of success!

Until we become humble in our own hearts we are not apt to profit greatly by the experiences and thoughts of others.

Sounds like a preachment on morality? Well, what if it does?

Even sermons, as dry and lacking in interest as they generally are, may be beneficial if they serve to reflect the shadow of our real selves so we may get an approximate idea of our smallness and superficiality.

Success in life is largely predicated upon who we know!

The best place to study the human animal is in your own mind, by taking as accurate an inventory as possible of *yourself.* When you know yourself thoroughly (if you ever do) you will also know much about others.

To know others, not as they seem to be, but as they really are, study them through:

* The posture of the body, and the way they walk
* The tone of the voice, its quality, pitch, volume
* The eyes, whether shifty or direct
* The use of words, their trend, nature, and quality

Through these open windows you may literally "walk right into a person's soul" and take a look at the *real human being!*

Going a step further, if you would know people study them:

* When angry
* When in love
* When money is involved

• When eating (alone, and unobserved, as they believe)

• When writing

• When in trouble

• When joyful and triumphant

• When downcast and defeated

• When facing catastrophe of a hazardous nature

• When trying to make a good impression on others

• When informed of another's misfortune

• When informed of another's good fortune

• When losing in any sort of a game of sport

• When winning at sport

• When alone, in a meditative mood

Before you can know people, as they really are, you must observe them in all the foregoing moods, and perhaps more, which is practically the equivalent of saying that you have no right to judge others at sight.

Appearances count, there can be no doubt of that, but appearances are often deceiving.

This course has been so designed that the student who masters it may take inventory of himself and of others by something more than "snap-judgment" methods. When you master this philosophy you will be able to look through the outer crust of personal adornment, clothes, so-called culture, and the like, and down deep into the heart.

This is a very broad promise!

It would not have been made if I had not known, from years of experimentation and analysis, that the promise can be met.

Some who have examined the manuscripts of this course have asked why it was not called a course in master salesmanship. The answer is that the word *salesmanship* is commonly associated with the marketing of goods or services, and it would, therefore, narrow down and circumscribe

NO PERSON IS EDUCATED

WHO HAS NOT AT LEAST

A SPEAKING ACQUAINTANCE

WITH THE LAW OF COMPENSATION,

AS IT IS DESCRIBED BY EMERSON.

the real nature of the course. It is true that this is a course in master salesmanship, providing one takes a deeper-than-the-average view of the meaning of salesmanship.

This philosophy is intended to enable those who master it to sell their way through life successfully, with the minimum amount of resistance and friction. Such a course, therefore, must help the student organize and make use of much truth that is overlooked by the majority of people who go through life as mediocrities.

Not all people are so constituted that they wish to know the truth about all matters vitally affecting life. One of the great surprises I met with, in connection with my research, is that so few people are willing to hear the truth when it shows up their own weaknesses.

We prefer illusions to realities!

New truths, if accepted at all, are taken with the proverbial grain of salt. Some of us demand more than a mere pinch of salt; we demand enough to pickle new ideas so they become useless.

For these reasons the introductory lesson of this course, and this lesson as well, cover subjects intended to pave the way for new ideas so those ideas will not be too severe a shock to the mind of the reader.

The thought I want to get across has been quite plainly stated by the editor of *The American Magazine* in an editorial that appeared in a recent issue, in the following words:

On a recent rainy night, Carl Lomen, the reindeer king of Alaska, told me a true story. It has stuck in my crop ever since. And now I am going to pass it along.

"A certain Greenland Eskimo," said Lomen, "was taken on one of the American North Polar expeditions a number of years ago. Later, as a reward for faithful service, he was brought to New York City for a short visit. At all the miracles of sight and sound he was filled with a most amazed wonder. When he returned to his native village he told stories of buildings that rose into the very face of the sky; of street cars, which he described as houses that moved along the trail, with people living in them as they moved; of mammoth bridges, artificial lights, and all the other dazzling concomitants of the metropolis.

"His people looked at him coldly and walked away. And forthwith throughout the whole village he was dubbed 'Sagdluk,' meaning 'the Liar,' and this name he carried in shame to his grave. Long before his death his original name was entirely forgotten.

"When Knud Rasmussen made his trip from Greenland to Alaska he was accompanied by a Greenland Eskimo named Mitek (Eider Duck). Mitek visited Copenhagen and New York, where he saw many things for the first time and was greatly impressed. Later, upon his return to Greenland, he recalled the tragedy of Sagdluk, and decided that it would not be wise to tell the truth. Instead, he would narrate stories that his people could grasp and thus save his reputation.

"So he told them how he and Doctor Rasmussen maintained a kayak on the banks of a great river, the Hudson, and how, each morning, they paddled out for their hunting. Ducks, geese, and seals were to be had aplenty, and they enjoyed the visit immensely.

"Mitek, in the eyes of his countrymen, is a very honest man. His neighbors treat him with rare respect."

The road of the truth-teller has always been rocky. Socrates sipping the hemlock, Christ crucified, Stephen stoned, Bruno burned at the stake, Galileo terrified into retraction of his starry truths—forever could one follow that bloody trail through the pages of history.

Something in human nature makes us resent the impact of new ideas.

We all hate to be disturbed in the beliefs and prejudices that have been handed down with the family furniture. At maturity too many of us go into hibernation and live off the fat of ancient fetishes. If a new idea invades our den we rise up snarling from our winter sleep.

The Eskimos, at least, had some excuse. They were unable to visualize the startling pictures drawn by Sagdluk. Their simple lives had been too long circumscribed by the brooding arctic night.

OPEN YOUR MIND

But there is no adequate reason why the average person should ever close his mind to fresh slants on life. He does, just the same. Nothing is more tragic—or more common—than mental inertia. For every ten people who are physically lazy there are ten thousand with stagnant minds. And stagnant minds are the breeding places of fear.

An old farmer up in Vermont always used to wind up his prayers with this plea: "Oh, God, give me an open mind!" If more people followed his example they might escape being hamstrung by prejudices. And what a pleasant place to live in the world would be.

Every person should make it his or her business to gather new ideas from sources other than the environment in which he or she daily lives and works.

The mind becomes withered, stagnant, narrow, and closed unless it searches for new ideas. The farmer should come to the city quite often, and walk among the strange faces and the tall buildings. He will go back to his farm, his mind refreshed, with more courage and greater enthusiasm.

City people should take a trip to the country every so often and freshen their minds with sights new and different from those associated with their daily routines.

Everyone needs a change of mental environment at regular periods, the same as a change and variety of food are essential. The mind becomes more alert, more elastic, and more ready to work with speed and accuracy after it has been bathed in new ideas, outside of one's own field of daily labor.

As a student of this course you will temporarily lay aside the set of ideas with which you perform your daily labors and enter a field of entirely new (and in some instances, heretofore unheard-of) ideas.

Splendid! You will come out, at the other end of this course, with a new stock of ideas which will make you more efficient, more enthusiastic, and more courageous, *no matter in what sort of work you may be engaged.*

Do not be afraid of new ideas. They may mean to you the difference between success and failure.

Some of the ideas introduced in this course will require no further explanation or proof of their soundness because they are familiar to practically everyone. Other ideas here introduced are new, and for that very reason many students of this philosophy may hesitate to accept them as sound.

I have thoroughly tested every principle described in this course, and the majority of the principles covered have been tested by scores of scientists and others who were quite capable of distinguishing between the merely theoretic and the practical.

For these reasons all principles here covered are known to be workable in the exact manner claimed for them. However, no reader of this book is asked to accept any statement made in these lessons without having first satisfied himself or herself, by tests, experiments, and analysis, that the statement is sound.

The major evil you are requested to avoid is that of forming opinions without definite *facts* as the basis, which brings to mind Herbert Spencer's famous admonition, in these words: "There is a principle which is a bar against all information; which is proof against all argument; and which cannot fail to keep a man in everlasting ignorance. This principle is contempt prior to examination."

It may be well to bear this principle in mind when you come to study the Law of the Master Mind described in these lessons. This law embodies an entirely new principle of mind operation, and, for this reason alone, it will be difficult for you to accept it as sound until after you have experimented with it.

When the fact is considered, however, that the Law of the Master Mind is believed to be the real basis of most of the achievements of those who are considered geniuses, this law takes on an aspect which calls for more than snap-judgment opinions.

It is believed by many scientists whose opinions on the subject have been given me that the Law of the Master Mind is the basis of practically all of the more important achievements resulting from group or cooperative effort.

The late Dr. Alexander Graham Bell said he believed the Law of the Master Mind, as it has been described in this philosophy, was not only sound, but that all the higher institutions of learning would soon be teaching that law as a part of their courses in psychology.

Charles P. Steinmetz said he had experimented with the law and had arrived at the same conclusion as that stated in these lessons, long before he talked to me about the subject.

Luther Burbank and John Burroughs made similar statements!

Edison was never questioned on the subject, but other statements of his indicate that he would endorse the law as being a possibility, if not in fact a reality.

Dr. Elmer Gates endorsed the law, when I spoke to him some years ago. Dr. Gates is a scientist of the highest order, ranking along with Steinmetz, Edison, and Bell.

I have talked to scores of intelligent businessmen who, while they were not scientists, admitted they believed in the soundness of the Law of the Master Mind. It is hardly excusable, therefore, for those of less ability to judge such matters, to form opinions as to this law, without serious, systematic investigation.

BY AND LARGE,

THERE IS NO SUCH THING

AS SOMETHING FOR NOTHING.

IN THE LONG RUN

YOU GET EXACTLY

THAT FOR WHICH YOU PAY,

WHETHER YOU ARE BUYING

AN AUTOMOBILE

OR A LOAF OF BREAD.

COMMENTARY

> *The Master Mind is a mental state that is developed through the harmonious co-operation of two or more people who ally themselves for the purpose of accomplishing any given task. The Master Mind harnesses the dedicated effort of a group of people, pools their resources, both tangible and intangible, and creates a new whole that is greater than the sum of its parts.*
>
> *A Master Mind operates (or should operate) among the members of the board of directors for huge international corporations. It operates among a team of engineers designing a new car. It operates in the production of a movie, the conduct of a political campaign, or the launch of a new advertising strategy. A Master Mind occurs when a church begins a fundraising program for a new building, when a group of neighbors organizes to increase the safety of their community, and when a young couple commits to a lifetime of marriage.*
>
> *A Master Mind is powerful and versatile. Its strength and broad usefulness arise from its connection to the fundamental principles around which our universe is organized.*

Let me lay before you a brief outline of what this lesson is and what it is intended to do for you!

Having prepared myself for the practice of law I will offer this introduction as a statement of my case. The evidence with which to back up my case will be presented in the seventeen lessons of which the course is composed.

The facts out of which this course has been prepared have been gathered through more than twenty-five years of business and professional experience, and my only explanation of the rather free use of the personal pronoun throughout the course is that I am writing from *first-hand experience.*

Before this course on the Law of Success was published, the manuscripts were submitted to two prominent universities with the request that they be read by competent professors with the object of eliminating or correcting any statements that appeared to be unsound, from an economic viewpoint.

This request was complied with and the manuscripts were carefully examined, with the result that not a single change was made with the exception of one or two slight changes in wording.

One of the professors who examined the manuscripts expressed himself, in part, as follows: "It is a tragedy that every boy and girl who enters high school is not efficiently drilled on the seventeen major parts of your course in the Law of Success. It is regrettable that the great university with which I am connected, and every other university, does not include your course as a part of its curriculum."

In as much as this course is intended as a map or blueprint that will guide you in the attainment of that coveted goal called success, may it not be well here to define success?

Success is the development of the power with which to get whatever one wants in life without interfering with the rights of others.

I would lay particular stress upon the word power because it is inseparably related to success. We are living in a world and during an age of intense competition, and the Law of the Survival of the Fittest is everywhere in evidence. Because of these facts all who would enjoy enduring success must go about its attainment through the use of power.

And what is *power?*

Power is *organized* energy or effort. This course is properly called the Law of Success for the reason that it teaches how one may organize *facts* and *knowledge* and the faculties of one's mind into a unit of power.

This course brings you a definite promise, namely:

That through its mastery and application you can get whatever you want, with but two qualifying words—"within reason."

This qualification takes into consideration your education, your wisdom or your lack of it, your physical endurance, your temperament, and all of the other qualities mentioned in the seventeen lessons of this course as being the factors most essential in the attainment of success.

Without a single exception those who have attained unusual success have done so, either consciously or unconsciously, through the aid of all or a portion of the seventeen major factors of which this course is compiled. If you doubt this statement, then master these seventeen lessons so you can go about the analysis with reasonable accuracy and analyze such men as Carnegie, Rockefeller, Hill, Harriman, Ford, and others of this type who have accumulated great fortunes of material wealth, and you will see that they understood and applied the principle of *organized effort* which runs, like a golden cord of indisputable evidence, throughout this course.

COMMENTARY

Anyone who has ever participated in a "Quality Circle" at work knows how business employs the Master Mind. The assembly teams that have replaced assembly lines at the most modern and efficient factories reflect the same use of the Master Mind.

Stephen Covey, the author of The 7 Habits of Highly Effective People *(Fireside), speaks of the Master Mind when he writes of "the interdependent person." "As an interdependent person . . ." he says, "I have access to the vast resources and potential of other human beings."*

Dennis Connor, the two-time winner of sailing's America's Cup, has a philosophy of teamwork that is a perfect expression of the Master Mind, emphasizing the power of commitment and dedication to a task. Read his book, The Art of Winning *(St. Martin's Press) for a vivid explanation of how Connor used the Master Mind to create a winning team.*

From restaurant kitchens to football teams, from factories to scientific laboratories, the Master Mind harnesses the potential power of a group of minds focused on a goal. Can you afford to ignore this valuable resource in your quest for success?

WHAT DO YOU MEAN BY SUCCESS?

Nearly twenty years ago I interviewed Mr. Carnegie for the purpose of writing a story about him. During the interview I asked him to what he attributed his *success*. With a merry little twinkle in his eyes he said:

"Young man, before I answer your question will you please define your term 'success'?"

After waiting until he saw that I was somewhat embarrassed by his request he continued: "By success you have reference to my money, have you not?" I assured him that money was the term by which most people measured success, and he then said: "Oh, well—if you wish to know how I got my money—if *that is what you call success*—I will answer your question by saying that we have a Master Mind here in our business, and that mind is made up of more than a score of men who constitute my personal staff of superintendents and managers and accountants and chemists and other necessary types. No one person in this group is the Master Mind of which I speak, but the sum total of the minds in the group, coordinated, organized and directed to a *definite* end in a spirit of harmonious cooperation is the power that got my money for me. No two minds in the group are exactly alike, but each man in the group does the thing that he is supposed to do and he does it better than any other person in the world could do it."

Then and there the seed out of which this course has been developed was sown in my mind, but that seed did not take root or germinate until later. This interview marked the beginning of years of research which led, finally, to the discovery of the principle of psychology described in the introductory lesson as the Master Mind.

I heard all that Mr. Carnegie said, but it took the knowledge gained from many years of subsequent contact with the business world to enable me to assimilate that which he said and clearly grasp and understand the principle back of it, which was nothing more nor less than the principle of *organized effort* upon which this course on the Law of Success is founded.

Carnegie's group of men constituted a Master Mind and that mind was so well organized, so well coordinated, so powerful, that it could have accumulated millions of dollars for Mr. Carnegie in practically any sort of endeavor of a commercial or industrial nature. The steel business in which that mind was engaged was but an incident in connection with the accumulation of the Carnegie wealth. The same wealth could have been accumulated had the Master Mind been directed in the coal business or the banking business or the grocery business, for the reason that back of the mind was *power*—that sort of power which *you* may have when you shall have organized the faculties of your own mind and allied yourself with other well-organized minds for the attainment of a Definite Chief Aim in life.

A careful check-up with several of Mr. Carnegie's former business associates, which was made after this course was begun, proves conclusively not only that there is such a law as that which has been called the Master Mind, but that this law was the chief source of Mr. Carnegie's success.

Perhaps no one was ever associated with Mr. Carnegie who knew him better than did Mr. C. M. Schwab. In the following words Mr. Schwab has very accurately described that "subtle something" in Mr. Carnegie's personality which enabled him to rise to such stupendous heights.

I never knew a man with so much imagination, lively intelligence, and instinctive comprehension. You sensed that he probed your thoughts and took stock of everything that you had ever done or might do. He seemed to catch at your next word before it was spoken. The play of his mind was dazzling and his habit of close observation gave him a store of knowledge about innumerable matters.

But his outstanding quality, from so rich an endowment, was the power of inspiring other men. Confidence radiated from him. You might be doubtful about something and discuss the matter with Mr. Carnegie. In a flash he would make you see that it was right and then absolutely believe it; or he might settle your doubts by pointing out its weakness. This quality of attracting others, then spurring them on, arose from his own strength.

IF YOU CAN RUN

A LOSING RACE WITHOUT

BLAMING YOUR LOSS

ON SOMEONE ELSE,

YOU HAVE BRIGHT

PROSPECTS OF SUCCESS

FURTHER DOWN

THE ROAD IN LIFE.

The results of his leadership were remarkable. Never before in history of industry, I imagine, was there a man who, without understanding his business in its working details, making no pretense of technical knowledge concerning steel or engineering, was yet able to build up such an enterprise.

Mr. Carnegie's ability to inspire others rested on something deeper than any faculty of judgment.

In the last sentence Mr. Schwab has conveyed a thought which corroborates the theory of the Master Mind to which I attributed the chief source of Mr. Carnegie's power.

Mr. Schwab has also confirmed the statement that Mr. Carnegie could have succeeded as well in any other business as he did in the steel business. It is obvious that his success was due to his understanding of his own mind and the minds of other men, and not to mere knowledge of the steel business itself.

This thought is most consoling to those who have not yet attained outstanding success, for it shows that success is solely a matter of correctly applying laws and principles which are available to all; and these laws, let us not forget, are fully described in the seventeen lessons of this course.

Mr. Carnegie learned how to apply the Law of the Master Mind. This enabled him to organize the faculties of his own mind and the faculties of other men's minds, and coordinate the whole behind a Definite Chief Aim.

Every strategist, whether in business or war or industry or other callings, understands the value of *organized,* coordinated effort. Every military strategist understands the value of sowing seeds of dissension in the ranks of the opposing forces, because this breaks up the power of coordination back of the opposition. During the First World War (and in every war since) much was heard about the effects of propaganda, and it seems not an exaggeration to say that the disorganizing forces of propaganda were much more destructive than were all the guns and explosives.

One of the most important turning points of the First World War came when the allied armies were placed under the direction of the French Marshall, Ferdinand Foch. There are well-informed military historians who claim that this was the move that spelled doom for the opposing armies.

Any modern railroad bridge is an excellent example of the value of *organized effort*, because it demonstrates quite simply and clearly how thousands of tons of weight may be borne by a comparatively small group of steel bars and beams so arranged that the weight is spread over the entire group.

There was a man who had seven sons who were always quarreling among themselves. One day he called them together and informed them that he wished to demonstrate just what their lack of cooperative effort meant. He had prepared a bundle of seven sticks that he had carefully tied together. One by one he asked his sons to take the bundle and break it. Each son tried, but in vain. Then he cut the strings and handed one of the sticks to each of his sons and asked him to break it over his knee. After the sticks had all been broken with ease, he said: "When you boys work together in a spirit of harmony you resemble the bundle of sticks, and no one can defeat you; but when you quarrel among yourselves anyone can defeat you one at a time."

There is a worthwhile lesson in this story of the man and his seven quarrelsome sons, and it may be applied to the people of a community, the employees and employers in a given place of employment, or to the state and nation in which we live.

Organized effort may be made a power, but it may also be a dangerous power unless guided with intelligence, which is the chief reason why the sixteenth lesson of this course is devoted largely to describing how to direct the power of organized effort so that it will lead to success; that sort of success which is founded upon truth and justice and fairness that leads to ultimate *happiness.*

One of the outstanding tragedies of this age of struggle and money madness is the fact that so few people are engaged in the effort which they like best. One of the objects of this course is to help each reader find his or her particular niche in the world's work, where both material prosperity and *happiness* in abundance may be found. To accomplish this purpose the various lessons of this course are skillfully designed to help you take inventory and find out what latent ability and hidden forces lie sleeping within.

This entire course is intended as a stimulus with which to enable you to see yourself and your hidden forces as they are, and to awaken in you the ambition and the vision and the determination to cause you to go forth and claim that which is rightfully yours.

Less than thirty years ago a man was working in the same shop with Henry Ford, doing practically the same sort of work that he was doing. It has been said that this man was really a more competent workman, in that particular sort of work, than Ford. Today this man is still engaged in the same sort of work, at wages of less than a hundred dollars a week, while Mr. Ford is the world's richest man.

What outstanding difference is there between these two men which has so widely separated them in terms of material wealth? Just this— Ford understood and applied the principle of *organized effort* while the other man did not.

In the little city of Shelby, Ohio, this principle of *organized effort* was applied for the purpose of bringing about a closer alliance between the churches and the business houses of a community.

The clergymen and businessmen formed an alliance, with the result that practically every church in the city was squarely back of every businessman, and every businessman is squarely back of every church. The effect was the strengthening of the churches and the business houses to such an extent that it has been said that it would be practically impossible for any individual member of either class to fail in his calling. The others who belong to the alliance will permit no such failures.

Here is an example of what may happen when groups form an alliance for the purpose of placing the combined power of the group back of each individual. The alliance has brought both material and moral advantages to the city of Shelby such as are enjoyed by but few other cities of its size in America. The plan has worked so effectively and so satisfactorily that a movement is now underway to extend it into other cities throughout America.

COMMENTARY

E. Colin Lindsey was a shoe salesman for the Belk Brothers store in Charlotte, North Carolina. There were many other clerks in that store, but Lindsey had the idea of proposing a new store in cooperation with the Belk family. Forty years later, he headed the thirty-five-store chain of Belk Lindsey department stores in the South, while the other salespeople he worked with still wondered what had happened. All that happened was that Lindsey applied organized effort and the others did not.

Jean Nidetch was one of millions of overweight people in America during the 1960s. She knew many other people who were in a similar position. But Nidetch realized how powerful it would be to bring those people together to inspire each other, to share experiences in losing weight, and so she founded Weight Watchers. From a first meeting with just fifty people, Weight Watchers grew into an organization of more than 1 million members—because Nidetch understood the importance of organized effort in helping others.

Alliances

That you may gain a still more concrete vision of just how this principle of *organized effort* can be made powerful, stop for a moment and allow your imagination to draw a picture of what would likely be the result if every church and every newspaper and every Rotary Club and every Kiwanis Club and every advertising club and every woman's club and every other civic organization of a similar nature, in your city, or in any other city in the United States should form an alliance for the purpose of pooling their power and using it for the benefit of all members of these organizations.

The results that might easily be attained by such an alliance stagger the imagination!

There are three outstanding powers in the world of *organized effort*. They are: the churches, the schools, and the newspapers. Think what might easily happen if these three great powers and molders of public opinion should ally themselves together for the purpose of bringing about any needed change in human conduct. They could, in a single generation, so modify the present standard of business ethics, for example, that it would practically be business suicide for any one to try to transact business under any standard except that of the Golden Rule. Such an alliance could be made to produce sufficient influence to change, in a single generation, the business, social, and moral tendencies of the entire civilized world. Such an alliance would have sufficient power to force upon the minds of the oncoming generations any ideals desired.

Power is *organized effort*, as has already been stated!

Success is based upon power!

That you may have a clear conception of what is meant by the term organized effort I have made use of the foregoing illustrations, and for the sake of further emphasis I am going to repeat the statement that the accumulation of great wealth and the attainment of any high station in life such as those that constitute what we ordinarily call success are based upon the vision to comprehend and the ability to assimilate and apply the major principles of the seventeen lessons of this course.

This course is in complete harmony with the principles of economics and the principles of applied psychology. You will observe that those lessons that depend, for their practical application, upon knowledge of psychology, have been supplemented with sufficient explanation of the psychological principles involved to render the lessons easily understood.

A GOOD ENCYCLOPEDIA

CONTAINS MOST

OF THE KNOWN FACTS

OF THE WORLD,

BUT THEY ARE AS USELESS

AS SAND DUNES UNTIL

ORGANIZED AND EXPRESSED

IN TERMS OF ACTION.

Before the manuscripts for this course went to the publisher they were submitted to some of the foremost bankers and businessmen of America, that they might be examined, analyzed, and criticized by the most practical type of mind. One of the best known bankers in New York City returned the manuscripts with the following comment:

"I hold a master's degree from Yale, but I would willingly exchange all that this degree has brought me in return for what your course on the Law of Success would have brought me had I been afforded the privilege of making it a part of my training while I was studying at Yale.

"My wife and daughter have also read the manuscripts, and my wife has named your course 'the master keyboard of life' because she believes that all who understand how to apply it may play a perfect symphony in their respective callings, just as a pianist may play any tune when once the keyboard of the piano and the fundamentals of music have been mastered."

No two people on earth are exactly alike, and for this reason no two people would be expected to attain from this course the same viewpoint. You should read the course, understand it, and then appropriate from it whatever you need to develop a well-rounded personality.

ANALYZE YOURSELF

Take your measure; make a self-analysis. (See the following commentary.) If you will answer all these questions truthfully, you will know more about yourself than the majority of people. Study the questions carefully, come back to them once each week for several months, and be astounded at the amount of additional knowledge of great value to yourself you will have gained by answering the questions truthfully. If you are not certain concerning the answers to some of the questions, seek the counsel of those who know you well, especially those who have no motive in flattering you, and see yourself through their eyes.

This book has been compiled for the purpose of helping you find out what are your natural talents, and for the purpose of helping organize, coordinate, and put into use the knowledge gained from experience. For more than twenty years I have been gathering, classifying, and organizing this material. During the past fourteen years I have analyzed more than 16,000 men and women, and all of the vital facts gathered from these analyses have been carefully organized and woven into this course. These analyses brought out many interesting facts that have helped to make this course practical and usable. For example, it was discovered that 95 percent of all who were analyzed were failures, and but 5 percent were successes. (By the term failure is meant that they had failed to find happiness and the ordinary necessities of life without struggle that was almost unbearable.) Perhaps this is about the proportion of successes and failures that might be found if all the people of the world were accurately analyzed. The struggle for a mere existence is tremendous among people who have not learned how to organize and direct their natural talents, while the attainment of those necessities, as well as the acquiring of many of the luxuries, is comparatively simple among those who have mastered the principle of *organized effort.*

One of the most startling facts brought to light by those 16,000 analyses was the discovery that the 95 percent who were classed as failures were in that class *because they had no Definite Chief Aim in life,* while the 5 percent constituting the successful ones not only had purposes that were *definite,* but they had, also, *definite plans* for the attainment of their purposes.

Another important fact disclosed by these analyses was that the 95 percent constituting the failures were engaged in work which they did not like, while the 5 percent constituting the successful ones were doing that which they liked best. It is doubtful whether a person could be a failure while engaged in work he liked best. Another vital fact learned from the analyses was that all of the 5 percent who were succeeding had formed the habit of systematic saving of money, while the 95 percent who were failures saved little. This is worthy of serious thought.

One of the chief objects of this course is to aid you in performing your chosen work in such a way that it will yield the greatest returns in both money and happiness.

COMMENTARY

Self-Analysis from Think and Grow Rich:

Do you often complain of "feeling bad?" If so, why?

Do you find fault with other people easily?

Do you often make mistakes in your work?

Are you sarcastic and obnoxious?

Do you deliberately avoid anyone? Why?

Does life seem futile and hopeless to you?

Do you often feel self-pity? If so, why?

Do you envy people who are more successful?

Do you devote more time to thinking about success or failure?

Are you gaining or losing self-confidence as you grow older?

Do you learn from your mistakes?

Are you permitting a relative or friend to worry you?

Are you sometimes elated and sometimes depressed?

Who is the most inspiring person you know?

Do you put up with negative influences?

Are you careless about your personal appearance?

Do you avoid your troubles by being busy?

Do you let other people do your thinking for you?

Are you annoyed by petty disturbances?

Do you resort to liquor, drugs, or cigarettes to calm you down?

Does anyone nag you?

Do you have an aim in life and a plan for achieving it?

Do you suffer from any of the six basic fears?

Do you have a way to shield yourself from the negative effects of others?

Do you actively attempt to keep your mind positive?

*What do you value more: your physical possessions or your ability to control your
own thoughts?*

Are you easily influenced by others?

Have you learned anything of value today?

Do you accept responsibility for problems?

Do you analyze mistakes and try to learn from them?

*Can you name your three most damaging weaknesses and explain what you are
doing to combat them?*

Do you encourage others to bring their troubles to you for sympathy?

Does your presence have a negative influence on others?

What habits in others annoy you the most?

Do you form your own opinions or let yourself be influenced by others?

Does your job inspire you?

Do you have spiritual forces powerful enough to keep you free from fear?

*If you believe that "birds of a feather flock together," what do you know about
your friends?*

Do you see any connection between your friends and some unhappiness in your life?

Is it possible that some close friend or associate has a negative influence on your mind?

What criteria do you use to determine who is helpful to you and who is harmful?

Are your intimate associates mentally superior or inferior to you?

How much time out of every day to you devote to:

- *your occupation?*
- *sleep?*
- *play and relaxation?*
- *acquiring useful knowledge?*
- *plain waste?*

Who among your friends and family:

- *encourages you the most?*
- *cautions you the most?*
- *discourages you the most?*

What is your greatest worry? Why do you tolerate it?

When others offer you unsolicited advice, do you accept it without question, or analyze their motive for giving it?

What, above all else, do you desire? Do you intend to get it? Are you willing to subordinate all other goals for this one? How much time do you devote to it daily?

Do you change your mind often?

Do you usually finish what you start?

Are you easily impressed by other people's business titles, college degrees, or wealth?

Are you often concerned about what other people might think or say of you?

Do you try to make friends with people because of their social status or wealth?

Whom do you believe to be the greatest person living? How is this person superior to you?

How much time have you devoted to studying and answering these questions?

At least one full day is needed to truly answer these questions and contemplate your answers. If you devote that time, you will know more about yourself than most people know of themselves.

A DEFINITE CHIEF AIM

The keynote of this entire lesson may be found in the word *definite.*

It is most appalling to know that 95 percent of the people of the world are drifting aimlessly through life, without the slightest conception of the work for which they are best fitted, and with no conception whatsoever of even the need of such a thing as a *definite* objective toward which to strive.

There is a psychological as well as an economic reason for the selection of a Definite Chief Aim in life. Let us devote our attention to the psychological side of the question first. It is a well-established principle of psychology that a person's acts are always in harmony with the dominating thoughts of his or her mind.

NO POSITION IN LIFE

CAN BE SECURE,

AND NO ACHIEVEMENT

CAN BE PERMANENT

UNLESS BUILT UP

ON TRUTH AND JUSTICE.

Any Definite Chief Aim that is deliberately fixed in the mind and held there, with the determination to realize it, finally saturates the entire subconscious mind until it automatically influences the physical action of the body toward the attainment of that purpose.

Your Definite Chief Aim in life should be selected with deliberate care, and after it has been selected it should be written out and placed where you will see it at least once a day, the psychological effect which is to impress this purpose upon your subconscious mind so strongly that it accepts that purpose as a pattern or blueprint that will eventually dominate your activities in life and lead you, step by step, toward the attainment of the object back of that purpose.

The principle of psychology through which you can impress your Definite Chief Aim upon your subconscious mind is called autosuggestion, or suggestion that you repeatedly make to yourself. It is a degree of self-hypnotism, but do not be afraid of it on that account, for it was this same principle through the aid of which Napoleon lifted himself from the lowly station of poverty-stricken Corsican to the dictatorship of France.

It is through the aid of this same principle that Thomas A. Edison has risen from a lowly beginning to become accepted as the leading inventor of the world. It was through the aid of this same principle that Lincoln bridged the mighty chasm between his lowly birth, in a log cabin in the mountains of Kentucky, and the presidency of the greatest nation on earth. It was through the aid of this same principle that Theodore Roosevelt became one of the most aggressive leaders that ever reached the presidency of the United States.

Autosuggestion

You need have no fear of the principle of autosuggestion as long as you are sure that the objective for which you are striving is one that will bring you happiness of an enduring nature. Be sure that your *definite purpose* is constructive; that its attainment will bring hardship and misery to no one; that it will bring you peace and prosperity, then apply, to the limit of your understanding, the principle of self-suggestion for the speedy attainment of this purpose.

On the street corner, just opposite the room in which I am writing, I see a man who stands there all day long and sells peanuts. He is busy every minute. When not actually engaged in making a sale he is roasting and packing the peanuts in little bags. He is one of that great army constituting the 95 percent who have no *definite purpose* in life. He is selling peanuts, not because he likes that work better than anything else he might do, but because he never sat down and thought out a *definite purpose* that would bring him greater returns for his labor. He is selling peanuts because he is a drifter on the sea of life, and one of the tragedies of his work is the fact that the same amount of effort that he puts into it, if directed along other lines, would bring him much greater returns.

Another one of the tragedies of this man's work is the fact that he is unconsciously making use of the principle of self-suggestion, but he is doing it to his own disadvantage. No doubt, if a picture could be made of his thoughts, there would be nothing in that picture except a peanut roaster, some little paper bags, and a crowd of people buying peanuts. This man could get out of the peanut business if he had the vision and the ambition first to imagine himself in a more profitable calling, and the perseverance to hold that picture before his mind until it influenced him to take the necessary steps to enter a more profitable calling. He puts sufficient labor into his work to bring him a substantial return if that labor were directed toward the attainment of a *definite purpose* that offered bigger returns.

One of my closest personal friends is one of the best-known writers and public speakers of this country. About ten years ago he caught sight of the possibilities of this principle of self-suggestion and began, immediately, to harness it and put it to work. He worked out a plan for its application that proved to be very effective. At that time he was neither a writer nor a speaker.

Each night, just before going to sleep, he would shut his eyes and see, *in his imagination,* a long council table at which he placed (in his imagination) certain well-known men whose characteristics he wished to absorb into his own personality. At the end of the table he placed Lincoln, and on either side of the table he placed Napoleon, Washington, Emerson, and Elbert Hubbard. He then proceeded to talk to these imaginary figures that he had seated at his imaginary council table, something after this manner:

Mr. Lincoln: I desire to build in my own character those qualities of patience and fairness toward all mankind and the keen sense of humor which were your outstanding characteristics. I need these qualities and I shall not be contented until I have developed them.

Mr. Washington: I desire to build in my own character those qualities of patriotism and self-sacrifice and leadership that were your outstanding characteristics.

Mr. Emerson: I desire to build in my own character those qualities of vision and the ability to interpret the laws of Nature as written in the rocks of prison walls and growing trees and flowing brooks and growing flowers and the faces of little children, which were your outstanding characteristics.

Napoleon: I desire to build in my own character those qualities of self-reliance and the strategic ability to master obstacles and profit by mistakes and develop strength out of defeat, which were your outstanding characteristics.

Mr. Hubbard: I desire to develop the ability to equal and even to excel the ability that you possessed with which to express yourself in clear, concise, and forceful language.

Night after night, for many months, this man saw these men seated around that imaginary council table until finally he had imprinted their outstanding characteristics upon his own subconscious mind so clearly that he began to develop a personality which was a composite of their personalities.

COMMENTARY

Napoleon Hill was by no means the first to encourage the use of autosuggestion. Perhaps the best-known advocate was French psychiatrist, Emil Coue. A contemporary of Freud in the late 1800s, Coue advocated the use of autosuggestion by the repetition of statements that he termed positive affirmations. He developed what he considered to be a perfect positive statement that was non-specific and could be used to improve any aspect of anyone's life. Coue instructed his patients to repeat the following phrase several times a day: "Every day in every way I am getting better and better." Word of his success with the method quickly spread, and the use of the phrase practically became a movement in Europe.

When Coue traveled to America on a lecture tour, the press of the day found his idea to be too simplistic and parodied his affirmation with their own version, "Hells bells, I'm well." It made Coue a laughingstock, and just as had happened when stage magicians cast doubt upon the efficacy of hypnosis, Coue's method of positive affirmation fell into disrepute.

Serious scientists and therapists continued to work with these methods, but as with Hill's theories about the power of the mind to heal the body, it took the open-ness of the latter part of the twentieth century before the techniques of self-hypnosis, autosuggestion, and positive affirmations began to gain general acceptance once again.

If you wish to increase your knowledge of these techniques, the following books will provide you with a diversity of information: Creative Vizualization *by* Shakti Gawain, Psycho-Cybernetics *by Dr. Maxwell Maltz,* Visualization: Directing the Movies of Your Mind *by Adelaide Bry,* Getting Well Again *by Dr. O. Carl Simonton,* Self-Hypnosis *by Leslie M. LeCron.*

The subconscious mind may be likened to a magnet, and when it has been vitalized and thoroughly saturated with any definite purpose it has a decided tendency to attract all that is necessary for the fulfillment of that purpose. Like attracts like, and you may see evidence of this law in every blade of grass and every growing tree. The acorn attracts from the soil and the air the necessary materials out of which to grow an oak tree.

It never grows a tree that is part oak and part poplar. Every grain of wheat that is planted in the soil attracts the materials out of which to grow a stalk of wheat.

It never makes a mistake and grows both oats and wheat on the same stalk.

People are subject, also, to this same Law of Attraction. Go into any cheap boardinghouse district in any city and there you will find people of the same general trend of mind associated together. On the other hand, go into any prosperous community and there you will find people of the same general tendencies associated together. Those who are successful always seek the company of others who are successful, while those who are on the ragged side of life always seek the company of those who are in similar circumstances. "Misery loves company."

Water seeks its level with no finer certainty than we all seek the company of those who occupy our own general status financially and mentally. A Yale University professor and an illiterate hobo have nothing in common. They would be miserable if thrown together for any length of time. Oil and water will mix as readily as will people who have nothing in common.

All of which leads up to this statement: you will attract to you people who harmonize with your own philosophy of life, whether you wish it or not. This being true, can you not see the importance of vitalizing your mind with a Definite Chief Aim that will attract to you people who will be of help to you and not a hindrance? Suppose your Definite Chief Aim is far above your present station in life. What of it? It is your privilege—in fact it is your *duty*, to aim high in life. You owe it to yourself and to the community in which you live to set a high standard for yourself.

There is much evidence to justify the belief that nothing *within reason* is beyond the possibility of attainment by the person whose Definite Chief Aim has been well developed. Some years ago Louis Victor Eytinge was given a life sentence in the Arizona penitentiary.

DO NOT "TELL" THE WORLD

WHAT YOU CAN DO—"SHOW" IT!

At the time of his imprisonment he was an all-around "bad man," by his own admissions. In addition to this it was believed that he would die of tuberculosis within a year.

Eytinge had reason to feel discouraged, if anyone ever had. Public feeling against him was intense and he did not have a single friend in the world who came forth and offered him encouragement or help.

Then something happened in his own mind that gave him back his health, put the dreaded disease to rout, and finally unlocked the prison gates and gave him his freedom. What was that "something"?

Just this: he made up his mind to whip the white plague and regain his health. That was a very Definite Chief Aim. In less than a year from the time the decision was made he had won. Then he extended that Definite Chief Aim by making up his mind to gain his freedom. Soon the prison walls melted from around him.

COMMENTARY

The details of this case are interesting. In prison, Louis Eytinge decided to become a writer. He took magazines, catalogs, and anything else that contained marketing copy, and he began to rewrite it. As his confidence in what he was doing grew, he sent the revised copy to the companies that had produced it. Some were not flattered, but others recognized that he had skill. Soon he was earning a good sum of money. But more important, his dedication impressed a group of his clients who decided to help him. They petitioned the governor of Arizona for clemency. It took some time, but Eytinge was freed and walked out of the prison and into a job with a public relations firm.

No undesirable environment is strong enough to hold the man or woman who understands how to apply the principle of autosuggestion in the creation of a Definite Chief Aim. Such a person can throw off the shackles of poverty; destroy the most deadly disease germs; rise from a lowly station in life to power and plenty.

All great leaders base their leadership upon a Definite Chief Aim. Followers are willing followers when they know that their leader is a person with a Definite Chief Aim who has the courage to back up that purpose with action. Even a balky horse knows when a driver with a Definite Chief Aim takes hold of the reins and yields to that driver. When a man with a Definite Chief Aim starts through a crowd everybody stands aside and makes a way for him, but let a man hesitate and show by his actions that he is not sure which way he wants to go and the crowd will step all over his toes and refuse to budge an inch out of his way.

Nowhere is the lack of a Definite Chief Aim more noticeable or more detrimental than it is in the relationship between parent and child. Children sense very quickly the wavering attitude of their parents and take advantage of that attitude quite freely. It is the same all through life—men with a Definite Chief Aim command respect and attention at all times.

COMMENTARY

In 1990 Douglas Grant was paralyzed in an accident that left him in a wheelchair. But instead of deciding that his life was over, Grant embarked on the pursuit of a Definite Chief Aim. His father had told him he would never walk again unless he had a vision in life. Grant's vision was not just to walk, but to win a gold medal as a weight lifter. "I decided I would make it happen," he says. He created his own strategy for rehabilitation that started to restore his mobility. By 1993 he was not only walking, he had won the World Championships of Powerlifting—getting that gold medal he had dreamed of.

But Grant's battle to restore his strength also excited his interest in nutrition. He created a Master Mind with a leading authority on enzymes, and developed an enzyme-activated nutritional system called Infinity2. The program is now used by such professional teams as the New York Yankees and the Houston Rockets, and Grant's company is doing millions of dollars of business each year.

The Definite Purpose and Finance

So much for the psychological viewpoint of a *definite purpose*. Let us now turn to the economic side of the question.

If a ship lost its rudder, in mid-ocean, and began circling around, it would soon exhaust its fuel supply without reaching shore, despite the fact that it would use up enough energy to carry it to shore and back several times.

The person who labors without a *definite purpose* that is backed up by a definite plan for its attainment resembles the ship that has lost its rudder. Hard labor and good intentions are not sufficient to carry anyone through to success, for how may any of us be sure that we have attained success unless it is established in our minds some definite object that we wish?

Every well-built house started in the form of a *definite purpose* plus a definite plan in the nature of a set of blueprints. Imagine what would happen if one tried to build a house by the haphazard method, without plans. Workmen would be in each other's way, building material would be piled all over the lot before the foundation was completed, and everybody on the job would have a different notion as to how the house ought to be built. Result, chaos and misunderstandings and cost that would be prohibitive.

Yet have you ever stopped to think that most people finish school, take up employment or enter a trade or profession without the slightest conception of anything that even remotely resembles a *definite purpose* or a definite plan? In view of the fact that science has provided reasonably accurate ways and means of analyzing character and determining the life work for which people are best fitted, does it not seem a modern tragedy that 95 percent of the adult population of the world is made up of men and women who are failures because they have not found their proper niches in the world's work?

If *success* depends upon power, and if power is *organized effort*, and if the first step in the direction of organization is a *definite purpose*, then one may easily see why such a purpose is essential.

Until you select a *definite purpose* in life you dissipate your energies and spread your thoughts over so many subjects and in so many different directions that they lead not to power, but to indecision and weakness.

With the aid of a magnifying glass you can teach yourself a great lesson on the value of *organized effort.* Through the use of such a glass you can focus the sun rays on a *definite* spot so strongly that they will burn a hole through a plank. Remove the glass (which represents the *definite purpose*) and the same rays of sun may shine on that same plank for a million years without burning it.

A thousand electric dry batteries, when properly organized and connected together with wires, will produce enough power to run a good-sized piece of machinery for several hours, but take those same cells singly, disconnected, and not one of them would exert enough energy to turn the machinery over once. The faculties of your mind might properly be likened to those dry cells. When you organize your faculties, according to the plan laid down in the seventeen lessons of this reading course on the Law of Success, and direct them toward the attainment of a *definite purpose* in life, you then take advantage of the cooperative or accumulative principle out of which *power* is developed, which is called organized effort.

Andrew Carnegie's advice was this: "Place all your eggs in one basket and then watch the basket to see that no one kicks it over." By that advice he meant, of course, that we should not dissipate any of our energies by engaging in sidelines. Carnegie was a sound economist and he knew that most people would do well if they so harnessed and directed their energies that some one thing would be done well.

When the plan back of this course was first born I remember taking the first manuscript to a professor of the University of Texas, and in a spirit of enthusiasm I suggested to him that I had discovered a principle that would be of aid to me in every public speech I delivered thereafter, because I would be better prepared to organize and marshal my thoughts.

He looked at the outline of the points for a few minutes, then turned to me and said:

"Yes, your discovery is going to help you make better speeches, but that is not all it will do. It will help you become a more effective writer, for I have noticed in your previous writings a tendency to scatter your thoughts. For instance, if you started to describe a beautiful mountain yonder in the distance you would be apt to sidetrack your description by calling attention to a beautiful bed of wild flowers, or a running brook, or a singing bird, detouring here and there, zigzag fashion, before finally arriving at the proper point from which to view the mountain. In the future you are going to find it much less difficult to describe an object, whether you are speaking or writing, because *your seventeen points represent the very foundation of organization.*"

A man who had no legs once met a man who was blind. He proposed to the blind man that they form an alliance that would be of great benefit to both. "You let me climb upon your back," said he to the blind man, "then I will use your legs and you may use my eyes. Between the two of us we will get along more rapidly."

COMMENTARY

Marty and Helen Shih are a brother and sister team that has proven the value of a Master Mind in turning organized effort into success. In 1979 they opened a flower stall on a street corner in Los Angeles. Their first day, they took in just $1.99.

Together they worked hard. One of their smartest decisions was to record as many details as possible about each of their customers. This allowed them to call and remind people of approaching birthdays, anniversaries, and special events— saving many a forgetful customer from embarrassment and earning the Shihs' enormous goodwill. From this simple start, the Shihs began compiling a valuable database. This value was increased by the fact that the Shihs were targeting the Asian-American community, one that many businesses had overlooked.

> *From there the Shihs developed a full-service referral company for new Asian immigrants, who can call and talk to operators who speak Mandarin, Cantonese, Korean, or Japanese. Internet web pages are available in the same languages. Their Asian American Association is allied with such major companies as DHL, New York Life, and Sprint, marketing services to a community that is often hard to reach. Annual sales are more than $200 million.*
>
> *The Shihs' simple venture into flower selling showed them an opportunity. Their dedicated, organized effort gave them the means to fill it. Now Fortune 500 companies are their allies in growing their business.*

Out of allied effort comes greater power. This is a point that is worthy of much repetition. The great fortunes of the world have been accumulated through the use of this principle of allied effort. That which one individual can accomplish single handed, during an entire lifetime, is but meager at best, no matter how well organized that individual may be, but that which one person may accomplish through the principle of alliance with others is practically without limitation.

That Master Mind to which Carnegie referred during my interview with him was made up of more than a score of minds. In that group were men of practically every temperament and inclination. Each man was there to play a certain part and he did nothing else. There was perfect understanding and teamwork among these men. It was Carnegie's business to keep harmony among them.

And he did it wonderfully well.

If you are familiar with team sports you know, of course, that the winning team is the one that best coordinates the efforts of its players. Teamwork wins. It is the same in the great game of life.

In your struggle for *success* you should keep constantly in mind the necessity of knowing what it is that you want—of knowing precisely what is your *definite purpose*—*and* the value of the principle of *organized effort* in the attainment of that which constitutes your *definite purpose*.

In a vague sort of way nearly everyone has a definite purpose, namely, the desire for *money!* But this is not a *definite purpose* within the meaning of the term as it is used in this lesson. Before your purpose could be considered *definite*, even though that purpose were the accumulation of money, you would have to reach a decision as to the precise method through which you intend to accumulate that money. It would be insufficient for you to say that you would make money by going into some sort of business. You would have to decide just what line of business. You would also have to decide just where you would locate. You would also have to decide the business policies under which you would conduct your business.

In answering the question, "What Is Your Definite Purpose in Life?" that appears in the questionnaire that I have used for the analysis of more than 16,000 people, many answered about as follows:

"My definite purpose in life is to be of as much service to the world as possible and earn a good living."

That answer is about as *definite* as a frog's conception of the size of the universe is accurate!

The object of this lesson is not to inform you as to what your life work should be, for indeed this could be done with accuracy only after you have been completely analyzed, but it is intended as a means of impressing upon your mind a clear conception of the value of a *definite purpose* of some nature, and of the value of understanding the principle of *organized effort* as a means of attaining the necessary power with which to materialize your *definite purpose.*

Careful observation of the business philosophy of more than one hundred men and women who have attained outstanding success in their respective callings disclosed the fact that each was a person of prompt and definite decision.

The habit of working with a Definite Chief Aim will breed in you the habit of prompt decision, and this habit will come to your aid in all that you do.

THE BEST COMPENSATION

FOR DOING THINGS

IS THE ABILITY TO DO MORE.

Moreover, the habit of working with a Definite Chief Aim will help you to concentrate all your attention on any given task until you have mastered it.

Concentration of effort and the habit of working with a Definite Chief Aim are two of the essential factors in success which are always found together. One leads to the other.

The best-known successful business leaders were all people of prompt decision who worked always with one main, outstanding purpose as a chief aim.

Some notable examples are as follows:

F. W. Woolworth chose as his Definite Chief Aim the belting of America with a chain of stores, and concentrated his mind upon this one task until he "made it and it made him."

William Wrigley concentrated on the production and sale of a five-cent package of chewing gum and turned this one idea into millions of dollars.

Thomas Edison concentrated upon the work of understanding physical laws and created more useful inventions than any other man who ever lived.

R. H. Ingersoll concentrated on a dollar watch and girdled the earth with them.

E. M. Statler concentrated on "homelike hotel-service" and made himself wealthy and useful to millions of people.

Woodrow Wilson concentrated on the White House for twenty-five years and became its chief tenant, because he knew the value of sticking to a Definite Chief Aim.

Abraham Lincoln concentrated his mind on freeing the slaves and became our greatest American President while doing it.

John D. Rockefeller concentrated on oil and became the richest man of his generation.

Henry Ford concentrated on cheap transportation for ordinary people and made himself the richest and most powerful man alive.

Andrew Carnegie concentrated on steel, made a great fortune, and plastered his name on public libraries throughout America.

King Gillette concentrated on a safety razor, gave the entire world a "close shave," and made himself a multimillionaire.

George Eastman concentrated on the Kodak camera and made the idea yield him a fortune while bringing much pleasure to millions of people.

William Randolph Hearst concentrated on sensational newspapers and made the idea worth millions of dollars.

Helen Keller concentrated on learning to speak, and, though she was deaf, dumb, and blind, realized her Definite Chief Aim.

Marshall Field concentrated on the world's greatest retail store and lo! it rose before him, a reality.

Philip Armour concentrated on the butchering business and established a great industry, as well as a big fortune.

The Wright brothers concentrated on the airplane and mastered the air.

George Pullman concentrated on the sleeping car and the idea made him rich and millions of people comfortable in travel.

Millions of people are concentrating, daily, on *poverty* and *failure* and getting both in overabundance.

COMMENTARY

There are many more examples:

Marie Curie concentrated on scientific investigation and was the first woman to win a Nobel Prize and the first person to ever win it twice.

Coco Chanel concentrated on elegant fashion and defined the way women dressed for a generation.

Henry Kaiser concentrated on building ships and built the American Navy during the Second World War.

Ray Kroc concentrated on hamburgers and made McDonalds the world's most successful restaurant.

Martin Luther King, Jr., concentrated on civil rights and led Americans of all colors forward.

Sam Walton concentrated on low prices and spread his stores across the country like a carpet.

George Lucas concentrated on Star Wars *and made it into the most successful movie franchise of all time.*

Stephen King concentrated on supernatural suspense novels and became the bestselling writer of his day.

Ted Turner concentrated on cable television and built an enormous media conglomerate.

Harry Helmsley concentrated on real estate and amassed more than $1 billion of land in New York City.

Martha Stewart concentrated on do-it-yourself projects, changed the way people thought about their homes, and created an empire of books, magazines, and television shows.

Bill Gates concentrated on software and became America's richest person.

Whom would you add?

Finding Your Life Work

Thus it will be seen that all who succeed work with some definite, outstanding aim as the object of their labors.

There is some one thing that you can do better than anyone else in the world could do it. Search until you find out what this particular line of endeavor is, make it the object of your Definite Chief Aim, and then organize all of your forces and attack it with the belief that you are going to win. In your search for the work for which you are best fitted, it will be well if you bear in mind the fact that you will most likely attain the greatest success by finding out what work you like best, for it is a well-known fact that a man generally best succeeds in the particular line of endeavor into which he can throw his whole heart and soul.

ANYONE CAN START

BUT ONLY THE THOROUGHBRED

WILL FINISH!

COMMENTARY

As with so much of what Hill wrote, his advice to focus on that for which you are best suited as your life's work has also been expanded upon by many other authors. It is the genesis of numerous bestsellers including Feel the Fear and Do It Anyway *by Susan Jeffers and* Wishcraft *by Barbara Sher with Annie Gotlieb.*

Let us go back, for the sake of clarity and emphasis, to the psychological principles upon which this lesson is founded, because it will mean a loss that you can ill afford if you fail to grasp the real reason for establishing a Definite Chief Aim in your mind. These principles are as follows:

First, every voluntary movement of the human body is caused, controlled, and directed by *thought*, through the operation of the mind.

Second, the presence of any thought or idea in your consciousness tends to produce an associated feeling and to urge you to transform that feeling into appropriate muscular action that is in perfect harmony with the nature of the thought.

For example, if you think of winking your eyelid and there are no counter influences or thoughts in your mind at the time to arrest action, the motor nerve will carry your thought from the seat of government, in your brain, and appropriate or corresponding muscular action takes place immediately.

Stating this principle from another angle: you choose, for example, a *definite purpose* as your life work and make up your mind that you will carry out that purpose. *From the very moment that you make this choice, this purpose becomes the dominating thought in your consciousness, and you are constantly on the alert for facts, information, and knowledge with which to achieve that purpose.* From the time that you plant a *definite purpose* in your mind, your mind begins, both consciously and unconsciously, to gather and store away the material with which you are to accomplish that purpose.

Desire is the factor that determines what your *definite purpose* in life shall be. No one can select your dominating *desire* for you, but once you select it yourself it becomes your Definite Chief Aim and occupies the spotlight of your mind until it is satisfied by transformation into reality, unless you permit it to be pushed aside by conflicting desires.

To emphasize the principle that I am here trying to make clear, I believe it not unreasonable to suggest that to be sure of successful achievement, one's Definite Chief Aim in life should be backed up with a burning desire for its achievement. I have noticed that boys and girls who enter college and pay their way through by working seem to get more out of their schooling than do those whose expenses are paid for them. The secret of this may be found in the fact that those who are willing to work their way through are blessed with a burning desire for education, and such a desire, if the object of the desire is within reason, is practically sure of realization.

Science has established, beyond the slightest room for doubt, that through the principle of autosuggestion any deeply rooted desire saturates the entire body and mind with the nature of the desire and literally transforms the mind into a powerful magnet that will attract the object of the desire, if it be within reason. For the enlightenment of those who might not properly interpret the meaning of this statement I will endeavor to state this principle in another way. For example, merely desiring an automobile will not cause that automobile to come rolling in, but, if there is a burning desire for an automobile, that desire will lead to the appropriate action through which an automobile may be paid for.

Merely desiring freedom would never release a prisoner if it were not sufficiently strong to cause him to do something to entitle himself to freedom.

Beyond Your Burning Desire

These are the steps leading from desire to fulfillment: first the burning desire, then the crystallization of that desire into a *definite purpose*, then sufficient appropriate *action* to achieve that purpose. *Remember that these three steps are always necessary to insure success.*

I once knew a very poor girl from a troubled family who had a *burning desire* for friends, and she finally got many of them, and a husband, too, but not without having transformed that desire into the development of a very attractive personality that, in turn, attracted other people.

I once had a *burning desire* to be able to analyze character accurately and that desire was so persistent and so deeply seated that it practically drove me into ten years of research and study of men and women.

George S. Parker makes one of the best fountain pens in the world, and despite the fact that his business is conducted from the little city of Janesville, Wisconsin, he has spread his product all the way around the globe and he has his pen on sale in every civilized country in the world. More than twenty years ago, Mr. Parker's *definite purpose* was established in his mind, and that purpose was to produce the best fountain pen that money could buy. He backed that purpose with a *burning desire* for its realization and if you carry a fountain pen the chances are that you have evidence in your own possession that it has brought him abundant success.

You are a contractor and builder, and, like those who build houses out of mere wood and brick and steel, you must draw up a set of plans after which to shape your success building. You are living in a wonderful age, when the materials that go into *success* are plentiful and cheap. You have at your disposal, in the archives of the public libraries [or on the Internet], the carefully compiled results of two thousand years of research covering practically every possible line of endeavor in which one would wish to engage. If you wish to become a member of clergy you have at hand the entire history of what has been learned by men and women who have preceded you in this field. If you want to become a mechanic you have at hand the entire history of the inventions of machines and the discovery and use of metals and metallic things in nature.

If you would become a lawyer you have at your disposal the entire history of law procedure. Through the Department of Agriculture, in Washington, you have at your disposal all that has been learned about farming and agriculture, where you may use it should you wish to find your life work in this field.

COMMENTARY

Here, as in many other places, Hill seems very far ahead of his time. In this passage, he anticipates the age of the Internet, recognizing that information may be the most valuable commodity any man or woman can possess.

The world was never so resplendent with *opportunity* as it is today. On every hand there is an ever-increasing demand for the services of the man or the woman who makes a better mousetrap or performs a better service or preaches a better sermon or digs a better ditch or runs a more accommodating bank.

This lesson will not be completed until you shall have made your choice as to what your Definite Chief Aim in life is to be and then recorded a description of that purpose in writing and placed it where you may see it every morning when you arise and every night when you retire.

Procrastination is . . . but why preach about it? You know that *you* are the hewer of your own wood and the drawer of your own water and the shaper of your own Definite Chief Aim in life; therefore, why dwell upon that which you already know?

A *definite purpose* is something that you must create for yourself. No one else will create it for you and it will not create itself. What are you going to do about it? and when? and how?

Desire

Start now to analyze your desires and find out what it is that you wish, then make up your mind to get it. Lesson Three will point out to you the next step and show you how to proceed. Nothing is left to chance, in this reading course. Every step is marked plainly. Your part is to follow the directions until you arrive at your destination, which is represented by your Definite Chief Aim. Make that aim clear and back it up with persistence that does not recognize the word *impossible*.

When you come to select your Definite Chief Aim just keep in mind the fact that you cannot *aim* too high.

Also keep in mind the never-varying truth that you'll get nowhere if you start nowhere. If your aim in life is vague, your achievements will also be vague, and it might well be added, very *meager. Know what you want, when you want it, why you want it, and how you intend to get it.* This is known to teachers and students of psychology as the WWWH formula—"what, when, why, and how."

Read this lesson four times, at intervals of one week apart.

You will see much in the lesson the fourth time you read it that you did not see the first time.

Your success in mastering this course and in making it bring you success will depend very largely, if not entirely, upon how well you follow *all* the instructions it contains.

Do not set up your own rules of study. Follow those laid down in the course, as they are the result of years of thought and experimentation. If you wish to experiment, wait until you master this course in the manner suggested by its author. You will then be in a position to experiment more safely. For the present, content yourself by being the student. You will, let us hope, become the teacher as well as the student, after you have followed the course until you have mastered it.

If you follow the instructions laid down in this course, you can no more fail than water can run uphill above the level of its source.

APPLYING THE PRINCIPLES OF THIS LESSON

Through the introductory lesson of this course you became familiar with the principle of psychology known as the Master Mind.

You are now ready to begin use of this principle as a means of transforming your *Definite Chief Aim* into reality. It must have occurred to you that one might as well have no *Definite Chief Aim* unless one has, also, a very definite and practical plan for making that aim become a reality.

EVERY LINE A MAN WRITES,

AND EVERY ACT

IN WHICH HE INDULGES,

AND EVERY WORD HE UTTERS,

SERVES AS INESCAPABLE EVIDENCE

OF THE NATURE OF THAT

WHICH IS DEEPLY IMBEDDED

IN HIS OWN HEART,

A CONFESSION

THAT HE CANNOT DISAVOW.

Your first step is to decide what your major aim in life shall be. Your next step is to write out a clear, concise statement of this aim. This should be followed by a statement, in writing, of the plan or plans through which you intend to attain the object of your aim.

COMMENTARY

Almost ten years later, when Hill wrote Think and Grow Rich, *he placed even greater emphasis on the need to write down your chief aim. And, as was mentioned earlier in this revised edition of* The Law of Success, *most of the self-improvement and motivational books written since agree that it is not enough for you to just know intellectually what you want, you must commit it to paper. If Hill believed the actual act was important, and if hundreds of other motivational experts agree, then you would be foolish not to follow this simple advice. Just do it.*

Your next and final step will be the forming of an alliance with some person or persons who will cooperate with you in carrying out these plans and transforming your *Definite Chief Aim* into reality.

The purpose of this friendly alliance is to employ the Law of the Master Mind in support of your plans. The alliance should be made between yourself and those who have your highest and best interests at heart. If you are married, your spouse should be one of the members of this alliance, providing there exists between you a normal state of confidence and sympathy. Other members of this alliance may be your mother, father, brothers or sisters, or some close friend or friends.

If you are a single person your sweetheart, if you have one, should become a member of your alliance. This is no joke—you are now studying one of the most powerful laws of the human mind, and you will serve your own best interests by seriously and earnestly following the rules laid down in this lesson, even though you may not be sure where they will lead you.

Those who join with you in the formation of a friendly alliance for the purpose of aiding you in the creation of a Master Mind should sign, with you, your statement of the object of your Definite Chief Aim. Every member of your alliance must be fully acquainted with the nature of your object in forming the alliance. Moreover, every member must be in hearty accord with this object and in full sympathy with you. Each member of your alliance must be supplied with a written copy of your statement of your Definite Chief Aim. With this exception, however, you are explicitly instructed to keep the object of your chief aim to yourself. The world is full of "Doubting Thomases" and it will do your cause no good to have these rattle-brained people scoffing at you and your ambitions. Remember, what you need is friendly encouragement and help, not derision and doubt.

If you believe in prayer you are instructed to make your Definite Chief Aim the object of your prayer at least once every twenty-four hours, and more often if convenient. If you believe there is a God who can and will aid those who are earnestly striving to be of constructive service in the world, surely you feel that you have a right to petition Him for aid in the attainment of what should be the most important thing in life to you.

If those who have been invited to join your friendly alliance believe in prayer, ask them, also, to include the object of this alliance as a part of their daily prayer.

Comes, now, one of the most essential rules that you *must follow.* Arrange with one or all of the members of your friendly alliance to state to you, in the most positive and definite terms at their command, that they know you can and will realize the object of your Definite Chief Aim. This affirmation or statement should be made to you at least once a day; more often if possible.

These steps must be followed persistently, with full faith that they will lead you where you wish to go! It will not suffice to carry out these plans for a few days or a few weeks and then discontinue them. *You must follow the described procedure until you attain the object of your Definite Chief Aim, regardless of the time required.*

From time to time it may become necessary to change the plans you have adopted for the achievement of the object of your Definite Chief Aim. Make these changes without hesitation. No human being has sufficient foresight to build plans that need no alteration or change.

If any member of your friendly alliance loses faith in the law known as the Master Mind, immediately remove that member and replace him or her with some other person.

Andrew Carnegie stated to me that he had found it necessary to replace some of the members of his Master Mind. In fact he stated that practically every member of whom his alliance was originally composed had, in time, been removed and replaced with some other person who could adapt himself more loyally and enthusiastically to the spirit and object of the alliance.

You cannot succeed when surrounded by disloyal and unfriendly associates, no matter what may be the object of your Definite Chief Aim. Success is built upon loyalty, faith, sincerity, cooperation, and the other positive forces with which one must surcharge his environment.

Many of you will want to form friendly alliances with those with whom you are associated professionally or in business, with the object of achieving success in your business or profession. In such cases the same rules of procedure which have been here described should be followed. The object of your Definite Chief Aim may be one that will benefit you individually, or it may be one that will benefit the business or profession with which you are connected. The Law of the Master Mind will work the same in either case. If you fail, either temporarily or permanently, in the application of this law, it will be for the reason that some member of your alliance did not enter into the spirit of the alliance with faith, loyalty, and sincerity of purpose.

The last sentence is worthy of a second reading!

The object of your Definite Chief Aim should become your hobby.

———————

"YES, HE SUCCEEDED . . .

BUT HE ALMOST FAILED!"

SO DID ROBERT FULTON

AND ABRAHAM LINCOLN

AND NEARLY ALL THE OTHERS

WHOM WE CALL SUCCESSFUL.

NO MAN EVER ACHIEVED

WORTHWHILE SUCCESS WHO DID NOT,

AT ONE TIME OR OTHER,

FIND HIMSELF WITH AT LEAST

ONE FOOT HANGING WELL OVER

THE BRINK OF FAILURE.

———————

You should ride this hobby continuously; you should sleep with it, eat with it, play with it, work with it, live with it, and *think* with it.

Whatever you want you may get if you want it with sufficient intensity, and keep on wanting it, providing the object wanted is one within reason, and you *actually believe you will get it!* There is a difference, however, between merely wishing for something and *actually believing* you will get it. Lack of understanding of this difference has meant failure to millions of people. The doers are the believers in all walks of life. Those who *believe* they can achieve the object of their Definite Chief Aim do not recognize the word *impossible.* Neither do they acknowledge temporary defeat. They *know* they are going to succeed, and if one plan fails they quickly replace it with another plan.

Every noteworthy achievement met with some sort of temporary setback before success came. Edison made more than ten thousand experiments before he succeeded in making the first talking machine record the words, "Mary had a little lamb."

If there is one word that should stand out in your mind in connection with this lesson, it is the word *persistence!*

You now have within your possession the key to achievement. You have but to unlock the door to the Temple of Knowledge and walk in. But you must go to the temple; it will not come to you. If these laws are new to you the going will not be easy at first. You will stumble many times, but keep moving! Very soon you will come to the brow of the mountain you have been climbing, and you will behold, in the valleys below, the rich estate of *knowledge* which shall be your reward for your faith and efforts.

Everything has a price. There is no such possibility as "something for nothing." In your experiments with the Law of the Master Mind you are jockeying with Nature, in her highest and noblest form. Nature cannot be tricked or cheated. She will give up to you the object of your struggles only after you have paid her price, which is *continuous, unyielding, persistent effort!*

What more could be said on this subject?

You have been shown *what to do, when to do it, how to do it,* and *why you should do it.* If you will master the next lesson, on self-confidence, you will then have the faith in yourself to enable you to carry out the instructions laid down for your guidance in this lesson.

> *Master of human destinies am I!*
> *Fame, love, and fortune on my footsteps wait.*
> *Cities and fields I walk; I penetrate*
> *Deserts and seas remote, and passing by*
> *Hovel and mart and palace—soon or late*
> *I knock, unbidden, once at every gate!*
> *If sleeping, wake—if feasting—rise before*
> *I turn away. It is the hour of fate,*
> *And they who follow me reach every state*
> *Mortals desire, and conquer every foe*
> *Save death; but those who doubt or hesitate,*
> *Condemned to failure, penury, and woe,*
> *Seek me in vain and uselessly implore.*
> *I answer not, and I return no more!*

—JOHN J. INGALLS

NEGLECTING TO BROADEN THEIR VIEW

HAS KEPT SOME MEN

DOING ONE THING ALL THEIR LIVES.

Lesson Three

Self-Confidence

AMIDST ALL THE MYSTERIES

BY WHICH WE ARE SURROUNDED,

NOTHING IS MORE CERTAIN THAN

THAT WE ARE IN THE PRESENCE

OF AN INFINITE AND ETERNAL ENERGY

FROM WHICH ALL THINGS PROCEED.

—Herbert Spencer

Lesson Three

SELF-CONFIDENCE

"You Can Do It If You Believe You Can!"

Before approaching the fundamental principles upon which this lesson is founded it will be of benefit to you to keep in mind the fact that it is practical—that it brings you the discoveries of more than twenty-five years of research—that it has the approval of the leading scientific men and women of the world who have tested every principle involved.

Skepticism is the deadly enemy of progress and self-development. You might as well lay this book aside and stop right here as to approach this lesson with the feeling that it was written by some theorist who had never tested the principles upon which the lesson is based.

Surely this is no age for the skeptic, because it is an age in which we have seen more of Nature's laws uncovered and harnessed than had been discovered in all past history of the human race. Within three decades we have witnessed the mastery of the air; we have explored the ocean; we have all but annihilated distances on the earth; we have harnessed the lightning and made it turn the wheels of industry; we have made seven blades of grass grow where but one grew before; we have instantaneous communication between the nations of the world. Truly, this is an age of illumination and unfoldment, but we have as yet barely scratched the surface of knowledge. However, when we shall have unlocked the gate that leads to the secret power which is stored up within us, it will bring us knowledge that will make all past discoveries pale into oblivion by comparison.

Thought is the most highly organized form of energy known to man, and this is an age of experimentation and research that is sure to bring us into greater understanding of that mysterious force called thought, which reposes within us. We have already found out enough about the human mind to know that one may throw off the accumulated effects of a thousand generations of *fear*, through the aid of the principle of *autosuggestion*. We have already discovered the fact that *fear* is the chief reason for poverty and failure and misery that takes on a thousand different forms. We have already discovered the fact that the person who masters *fear* may march on to successful achievement in practically any undertaking, despite all efforts to defeat him.

The development of *self-confidence* starts with the elimination of this demon called *fear*, which sits upon a man's shoulder and whispers into his ear: "You can't do it—you are afraid to try—you are afraid of public opinion—you are afraid that you will fail—you are afraid you have not the ability."

This *fear* demon is getting into close quarters. Science has found a deadly weapon with which to put it to flight, and this lesson on *self-confidence* has brought you this weapon for use in your battle with the world-old enemy of progress, *fear*.

THE SIX BASIC FEARS OF MANKIND

Every person falls heir to the influence of six basic fears. Under these six fears may be listed the lesser fears. The six basic or major fears are here enumerated and the sources from which they are believed to have grown are described. The six basic fears are:

* The fear of poverty
* The fear of old age
* The fear of criticism
* The fear of loss of love of someone
* The fear of ill health
* The fear of death

Study the list, then take inventory of your own fears and ascertain under which of the six headings you can classify them.

Every human being who has reached the age of understanding is bound down, to some extent, by one or more of these six basic fears. As the first step in the elimination of these six evils let us examine the sources from whence we inherited them.

Physical and Social Heredity

All that man is, both physically and mentally, he came by through two forms of heredity. One is known as physical heredity and the other is called social heredity.

Through the law of physical heredity man has slowly evolved from the ameba (a single-cell animal form), through stages of development corresponding to all the known animal forms now on this earth, including those which are known to have existed but which are now extinct.

Every generation through which man has passed has added to his nature something of the traits, habits, and physical appearance of that generation. Our physical inheritance, therefore, is a heterogeneous collection of many habits and physical forms.

There seems little, if any, doubt that while the six basic human fears could not have been inherited through physical heredity (these six basic fears being mental states of mind and therefore not capable of transmission through physical heredity), it is obvious that through physical heredity a most favorable lodging place for these six fears has been provided.

By far the most important part of a person's make-up comes to him through the Law of Social Heredity, this term having reference to the methods by which one generation imposes upon the minds of the generation under its immediate control the superstitions, beliefs, legends, and ideas which it, in turn, inherited from the generation preceding.

The term social heredity should be understood to mean any and all sources through which a person acquires knowledge, such as schooling of religious and all other natures, reading, word of mouth conversation, story telling, and all manner of thought inspiration coming from personal experiences.

Through the operation of the Law of Social Heredity anyone having control of the mind of a child may, through intense teaching, plant in that child's mind any idea, whether false or true, in such a manner that the child accepts it as true and it becomes as much a part of the child's personality as any cell or organ of its physical body (and just as hard to change in its nature).

It is through the Law of Social Heredity that the religionist plants in the child's mind dogmas and creeds and religious ceremonies too numerous to describe, holding those ideas before that mind until the mind accepts them and forever seals them as a part of its irrevocable belief.

The mind of a child which has not come into the age of general understanding, during an average period covering, let us say, the first two years of its life, is plastic, open, clean, and free. Any idea planted in such a mind by one in whom the child has confidence takes root and grows, so to speak, in such a manner that it never can be eradicated or wiped out, no matter how opposed to logic or reason that idea may be.

Many religionists claim that they can so deeply implant the tenets of their religion in the mind of a child that there never can be room in that mind for any other religion, either in whole or in part. The claims are not greatly overdrawn.

With this explanation of the manner in which the Law of Social Heredity operates you will be ready to examine the sources from which humans inherit the six basic fears. Moreover, any reader (except those who have not yet grown big enough to examine truth that steps upon the "pet corns" of their own superstitions) may check the soundness of the principle of social heredity as it is here applied to the six basic fears, without going outside of his or her own personal experiences.

Fortunately, practically the entire mass of evidence submitted in this lesson is of such a nature that all who sincerely seek the truth may ascertain, for themselves, whether the evidence is sound or not.

For the moment at least, lay aside your prejudices and preconceived ideas (you may always go back and pick them up again, you know) while we study the origin and nature of man's six worst enemies, the six basic fears.

COMMENTARY

Hill continued to reexamine the six fears throughout his life. His discussion of them appears in several variations. It appears first in the original version of The Law of Success, published in pamphlet form. There, in the Lesson One Appendix, he lists the fears in a different order. Fear of ill health comes third and fear of criticism fifth; here their positions are reversed.

In Think and Grow Rich, he lists poverty, criticism, and ill health as the primary fears, saying that they are at the bottom of one's worries. Here one sees the reason for his fascination with the subject. "Indecision is the seedling of fear," he says. "Indecision crystallizes into doubt and the two become fear." Fear, then, becomes a symptom of the thought and action Hill shows us how to reform.

His commentaries differ also. The most significant departures are noted following.

REMEMBER THAT WHEN YOU

MAKE AN APPOINTMENT

WITH ANOTHER PERSON

YOU ASSUME THE RESPONSIBILITY

OF PUNCTUALITY, AND

THAT YOU HAVE NOT THE RIGHT

TO BE A SINGLE MINUTE LATE.

The Fear of Poverty

It requires courage to tell the truth about the origins of this fear, and still greater courage, perhaps, to accept the truth after it has been told. The fear of poverty grew out of man's inherited tendency to prey upon his fellow man economically. Nearly all forms of lower animals have instinct but appear not to have the power to reason and think; therefore, they prey upon one another physically. We, with our superior sense of intuition, thought, and reason, do not eat our fellow human beings bodily; we get more satisfaction out of eating others *financially!*

Of all the ages of the world of which we know anything, the age in which we live seems to be the age of money worship. A person is considered less than the dust of the earth unless he can display a fat bank account. Nothing brings us so much suffering and humiliation as does *poverty*. No wonder we *fear* poverty. Through a long line of inherited experiences with others like us we have learned, for certain, that this animal cannot always be trusted where matters of money and other evidences of earthly possessions are concerned.

Many marriages have their beginning (and oftentimes their ending) solely on the basis of the wealth possessed by one or both of the contracting parties. It is no wonder that the divorce courts are busy!

"Society" could quite properly be spelled "$ociety," because it is inseparably associated with the dollar mark. So eager are we to possess wealth that we will acquire it in whatever manner we can; through legal methods, if possible, through other methods if necessary.

The fear of poverty is a terrible thing!

A man may commit murder, engage in robbery, rape, and all other manner of violation of the rights of others and still regain a high station in the minds of people of his society, *providing* always that he does not lose his wealth. Poverty, therefore, is a crime—an unforgivable sin, as it were.

No wonder we fear it!

Every statute book in the world bears evidence that the fear of poverty is one of the six basic fears of mankind, for in every such book of laws may be found various and sundry laws intended to protect the weak from the strong. To spend time trying to prove either that the fear of poverty is one of man's inherited fears, or that this fear has its origin in man's nature to cheat his fellow man, would be similar to trying to prove that three times two are six.

COMMENTARY FROM THE CHAPTER ONE APPENDIX

"Humans are such great an offenders in this respect that nearly every state and nation has been obliged to pass laws, scores of laws, to protect the weak from the strong. Every code of laws ever written provides indisputable evidence of humanity's nature to prey upon its weaker members economically."

In Think and Grow Rich *Hill lists six symptoms of the fear of poverty: indifference (lack of ambition, laziness, etc.); indecision; doubt (expressed through alibis and excuses; worrying (expressed through fault finding; overcaution (shown in general negativity); and procrastination.*

Obviously no one would ever fear poverty if we had any grounds for trusting our fellow men, for there is food and shelter and raiment and luxury of every nature sufficient for the needs of every person on earth, and all these blessings would be enjoyed by every person except for the swinish habit that humans have of trying to push all the other swine out of the trough, even after everyone has all and more than needed.

The Fear of Old Age

In the main this fear grows out of two sources. First, the thought that old age may bring with it *poverty*. Secondly, human beings have learned to fear old age because it meant the approach of another, and possibly a much more horrible, world than this one which is known to be bad enough.

In the basic fear of old age humans have two very sound reasons for their apprehension: the one growing out of distrust of those who may seize whatever worldly goods we may possess, and the other arising from the terrible pictures of the world to come which were deeply planted in our minds, through the Law of Social Heredity, long before any of us came into possession of that mind.

Is it any wonder that so many fear the approach of old age?

The Fear of Criticism

Just how humans acquired this basic fear it would be hard, if not impossible, definitely to determine, but one thing is certain, we all have it in well-developed form.

I am inclined to attribute the basic fear of criticism to that part of our inherited nature that prompts many of us not only to take away our fellow human's goods and wares but to justify our actions by *criticism* of the character of others.

The fear of criticism takes on many different forms, the majority of which are petty and trivial in nature, even to the extent of being childish in the extreme.

The makers of all manner of clothing have not been slow to capitalize on this basic fear of criticism with which all humankind is cursed. Every season, it will be observed, the styles in many articles of wearing apparel change. Who establishes the styles? Certainly not the purchaser of clothes, but the manufacturer of clothes. Why does he change the styles so often? Obviously this change is made so that the manufacturer can sell more clothes.

For the same reason the manufacturers of automobiles (with a few rare and very sensible exceptions) change styles every season.

The manufacturer of clothing knows how the human animal fears to wear a garment that is one season out of step with what they are all wearing now.

Is this not true? Does not your own experience back it up?

Powerful and mighty is the fear of criticism.

IN EVERY SOUL

THERE HAS BEEN DEPOSITED

THE SEED OF A GREAT FUTURE,

BUT THAT SEED

WILL NEVER GERMINATE,

MUCH LESS GROW TO MATURITY,

EXCEPT THROUGH THE RENDERING

OF USEFUL SERVICE.

COMMENTARY

From Think and Grow Rich: "The fear of criticism robs man of his initiative, destroys his power of imagination, limits his individuality, takes away his self-reliance, and does him damage in a hundred other ways. Parents often do their children irreparable injury by criticizing them. . . . It should be recognized as a crime (in reality it is a crime of the worst nature), for any parent to build an inferiority complex in the mind of a child, through unnecessary criticism. Employers who understand human nature get the best there is in employees, not by criticism but by constructive suggestion."

The Fear of Loss of Love of Someone

The source from which this fear originated needs but little description, for it is obvious that it grew out of man's nature to steal his fellow man's mate; or at least to take liberties with her.

There can be but little doubt that jealousy and all other similar forms of more or less mild dementia praecox (insanity) grew out of the fear we all inherited of the loss of love of someone.

Of all the sane fools I studied, the jealous lover is the oddest and strangest. Fortunately, I had personal experience of this form of insanity, but from that experience I learned that the fear of the loss of love of someone is one of the most painful, if not in fact the most painful, of all the six basic fears. And it seems reasonable to add that this fear plays more havoc with the human mind than do any of the other six basic fears of mankind, often leading to the more violent forms of permanent insanity.

COMMENTARY

From the Appendix to Lesson One: "This fear fills the asylums with the insanely jealous, for jealousy is nothing but a form of insanity. It also fills the divorce courts and causes murders and other forms of cruel punishment. It is a holdover, handed down through social heredity, from the Stone Age when man preyed upon his fellow man *by stealing his mate by physical force. The method, but not the practice, has now changed to some extent. Instead of physical force man now steals his fellow man's mate with pretty colorful ribbons and fast motor cars and bootleg whisky and sparkling rocks and stately mansions."*

The Fear of Ill Health

This fear has its origin, to considerable extent also, in the same sources from which the fears of poverty and old age are derived.

The fear of ill health is closely associated with both poverty and old age, because it also leads toward the borderline of terrible worlds which people know little of, but about which there are many discomforting stories.

I strongly suspect that those engaged in the business of selling good health methods have had considerable to do with keeping the fear of ill health alive in the human mind.

For longer than the record of the human race can be relied upon, the world has known of various and sundry forms of therapy and health purveyors. If a person gains a living from keeping others in good health it seems natural that he or she would use every possible means to persuade them of the need for caregiving services. Thus, in time, it might be that people would inherit a fear of ill health.

COMMENTARY

From the Appendix to Lesson One: "This fear is born of both physical and social heredity. From birth until death there is eternal warfare within every physical body; warfare between groups of cells, one group being known as the friendly builders of the body, and the other as the destroyers, or "disease germs." The seed of fear is born in the physical body to begin with, as the result of nature's cruel plan of permitting the stronger forms of cell life to prey upon the weaker. Social heredity has played its part though lack of cleanliness and knowledge of sanitation. Also, through the law of suggestion cleverly manipulated by those who profited by ill health."

> *In* Think and Grow Rich *Hill suggests that ill health comes from fear: "Thought impulses immediately begin to translate themselves into their physical equivalent, whether those thoughts are voluntary or involuntary.... All thought has a tendency to clothe itself in its physical equivalent."*

The Fear of Death

To many this is the worst of all the six basic fears, and the reason why it is so regarded becomes obvious to even the casual student of psychology.

The terrible pangs of fear associated with death may be charged directly to religious fanaticism, the source that is more responsible for it than are all other sources combined.

So-called heathens are not as much afraid of *death* as are the civilized, especially that portion of the civilized population that has come under the influence of theology.

For hundreds of millions of years we have been asking the still unanswered (and, it may be, the unanswerable) questions, *whence?* and *whither? Where did I come from and where am I going after death?*

The more cunning and crafty, as well as the honest but credulous, of the race have not been slow to offer the answer to these questions. In fact the answering of these questions has become one of the so-called learned professions, despite the fact that but little learning is required to enter this profession.

Witness, now, the major source of origin of the fear of *death!*

"Come into my tent, embrace my faith, accept my dogmas (and pay my salary) and I will give you a ticket that will admit you straightway into heaven when you die," says the leader of one form of sectarianism. "Remain out of my tent," says this same leader, "and you will go direct to hell, where you will burn throughout eternity."

While, in fact, the self-appointed leader may not be able to provide safe-conduct into heaven nor, by lack of such provision, allow the unfortunate seeker after truth to descend into hell, the possibility of the latter seems so terrible that it lays hold of the mind and creates that fear of fears, the fear of *death!*

In truth no one knows, and no one has ever known, what heaven or hell is like, or if such places exist, and this very lack of definite knowledge opens the door of the human mind to the charlatan to enter and control that mind with his stock of legerdemain and various brands of trickery, deceit, and fraud.

The truth is this—nothing less and nothing more—*no person knows nor has any person ever known where we come from at birth or where we go at death.* Any one claiming otherwise is either deceiving himself or he is a conscious impostor who makes it a business to live without rendering service of value, while preying upon the credulity of humanity.

Be it said, in their behalf, however, the majority of those engaged in selling tickets into heaven actually believe not only that they know where heaven exists, but that their creeds and formulas will give safe passage to all who embrace them.

This belief may be summed up in one word—*credulity!*

Religious leaders, generally, make the broad, sweeping claim that the present civilization owes its existence to the work done by the churches. I am willing to grant their claims to be correct if, at the same time, I am permitted to add that even if this claim be true the theologians haven't a great deal to brag about.

But it is not—cannot be—true that civilization has grown out of the efforts of the organized churches and creeds, if by the term civilization is meant the uncovering of the natural laws and the many inventions to which the world is the present heir.

If the theologians wish to claim for themselves that part of civilization that has to do with man's conduct toward his fellow man, they are perfectly welcome to it, as far as I am concerned; but, on the other hand, if they presumed to gobble up the credit for all the scientific discovery of mankind I would protest vigorously.

COMMENTARY

You can make and put into action a plan of attack on fear.

Ask yourself which of the six basic fears is doing you the greatest damage. We are slowly discovering more about these six basic fears. The most effective tool with which to fight them is organized knowledge. Ignorance and fear are twins. They are generally found together. But for ignorance, the six basic fears would disappear from human thought. In every public library you can find the remedy for these six enemies.

Begin with Ralph Waldo Emerson's "Essay on Compensation." Then select some of the previously mentioned books on self-suggestion and inform yourself about the principle through which your beliefs of today become the realities of tomorrow.

Through the principle of social heredity, the ignorance and superstition of the past have been passed on to you. But you are living in a modern age. On every hand you may see evidence that every effect has a natural cause. Begin, now, to study effects by their causes and soon you will emancipate your mind from the burden of the six basic fears.

Begin by selecting two people whom you know close at hand; one should represent your idea of failure and the other should correspond to your idea of success. Find out what made one a failure and the other a success. Get the real facts. In the process of gathering these facts you will have taught yourself a great lesson on cause and effect.

Nothing ever just happens. In a single month of properly directed self-suggestion you may place your foot upon the neck of every one of your six basic fears. In twelve months of persistent effort you may drive the entire herd into the corner where it will never again do you any serious injury.

You will resemble tomorrow the dominating thoughts that you keep alive in your mind today! Plant in your mind the seed of determination to whip your six basic fears and the battle will have been half won then and there. Keep this intention in your mind and it will slowly push your six worst enemies out of sight, as they exist nowhere except in your own mind.

A person who is powerful fears nothing; not even God. The powerful person loves God, but fears Him never! Enduring power never grows out of fear. Any power that is built upon fear is bound to crumble and disintegrate. Understand this great truth and you will never be so unfortunate as to try to raise yourself to power through the fears of other people who may owe you temporary allegiance.

HOW LESSONS ARE LEARNED

It is hardly sufficient to state that social heredity is the method through which humans gather all knowledge that reaches us through the five senses. It is more to the point to state *how* social heredity works, in as many different applications as will give you a comprehensive understanding of that law.

COMMENTARY

Appropriately enough, Hill here turns to animal stories as a way of discussing the development of human character. Hill's frequent references to Nature's Bible demonstrate that he believed human beings are a part of Nature. But he also values the importance of the human social environment in weighing in on the relative influences of Nature and nurture, Hill uses the term physical heredity *for what we today might call* genetic predisposition. *By* social heredity *he means what we might call, simply,* conditioning *or* social conditioning *or* socialization.

The Law of Social Heredity

Let us begin with some of the lower forms of animal life and examine the manner in which they are affected by the Law of Social Heredity.

COMMENTARY

Many authors and lecturers of Napoleon Hill's day prided themselves on being storytellers, and they often drew upon the natural world for examples around

which to spin a yarn that would entertain while conveying the points they were try-
ing to make. However, the America in which most of us live today is not nearly as
bucolic as the one in which Hill grew up. There's a lot less catching of frogs in the
creek or watching of grouse in the fields, and kids think chickens come as a half-
dozen thighs or breasts shrink-wrapped in a package from the supermarket.

For that reason, as this edition was being prepared, there was considerable
discussion among the editors about the inclusion of Hill's animal analogies. It was
concluded that the points made are as valid today as they were when Hill wrote
them, and though they might be considered quaint by the modern reader, the sto-
ries themselves provide interesting insights into the life and times of Napoleon Hill.

Shortly after I began to examine the major sources from which we gather the knowledge that makes us what we are, some thirty-odd years ago, I discovered the nest of a ruffed grouse. The nest was so located that the mother bird could be seen from a considerable distance when she was on the nest. With the aid of a pair of field glasses I watched the bird closely until the young birds were hatched out. It happened that the regular daily observation was made but a few hours after the young birds came out of the shell. Desiring to know what would happen, I approached the nest. The mother bird remained nearby until I was within ten or twelve feet of her, then she disarranged her feathers, stretched one wing over her leg, and went hobbling away, making a pretense of being crippled. Being somewhat familiar with the tricks of mother birds, I did not follow, but, instead, went to the nest to take a look at the little ones. Without the slightest signs of fear they turned their eyes toward me, moving their heads first one way and then another. I reached down and picked one of them up. With no signs of fear it stood in the palm of my hand. I laid the bird back in the nest and went away to a safe distance to give the mother bird a chance to return.

The wait was short. Very soon she began cautiously to edge her way back toward the nest until she was within a few feet of it, when she spread her wings and ran as fast as she could, uttering, meanwhile, a

YOU ARE FORTUNATE

IF YOU HAVE LEARNED

THE DIFFERENCE BETWEEN

TEMPORARY DEFEAT AND FAILURE;

MORE FORTUNATE STILL,

IF YOU HAVE LEARNED

THE TRUTH THAT THE VERY

SEED OF SUCCESS IS DORMANT

IN EVERY DEFEAT

THAT YOU EXPERIENCE.

series of sounds similar to those of a hen when she has found some morsel of food and wishes to call her brood to partake of it.

She gathered the little birds around and continued to quiver in a highly excited manner, shaking her wings and ruffling her feathers. One could almost hear her words as she gave the little birds their first lesson in self-defense, through the Law of Social Heredity.

"You silly little creatures! Do you not know that humans are your enemies? Shame on you for allowing that man to pick you up in his hands. It's a wonder he didn't carry you off and eat you alive! The next time you see a man approaching make yourselves scarce. Lie down on the ground, run under leaves, go anywhere to get out of sight, and remain out of sight until the enemy is well on his way."

The little birds stood around and listened to the lecture with intense interest. After the mother bird had quieted down I again started to approach the nest. When within twenty feet or so of the guarded household the mother bird again started to lead me in the other direction by crumpling up her wing and hobbling along as if she were crippled. I looked at the nest, but the glance was in vain. The little birds were nowhere to be found! They had learned rapidly to avoid their natural enemy, thanks to their natural instinct.

Again I retreated, waited until the mother bird had reassembled her household, then came out to visit them, but with similar results. When I approached the spot where I last saw the mother bird, not the slightest signs of the little fellows were to be found.

When a small boy I captured a young crow and made a pet of it. The bird became quite well satisfied with its domestic surroundings and learned to perform many tricks requiring considerable intelligence. After the bird was big enough to fly it was permitted to go wherever it pleased. Sometimes it would be gone for many hours, but it always returned home before dark.

One day some wild crows became involved in a fight with an owl in a field near the house where the pet crow lived. As soon as the pet heard the "caw, caw, caw" of its wild relatives it flew up on top of the house, and with signs of great agitation walked from one end of the house to the other. Finally it took wing and flew in the direction of the battle. I followed to see what would happen. In a few minutes I found the pet sitting on the lower branches of a tree. Two wild crows were on a limb just above, chattering and walking back and forth, acting very much in the same fashion that angry parents behave toward their offspring when chastising them.

As I approached, the two wild crows flew away, one of them circling around the tree a few times, meanwhile letting out a terrible flow of most abusive language, which, no doubt, was directed at its foolish relative who hadn't enough sense to fly while the flying was good.

The pet was called, but it paid no attention. That evening it returned home, but would not come near the house. It sat on a high limb of an apple tree and talked in crow language for about ten minutes, saying, no doubt, that it had decided to go back to the wild life of its fellows. It then flew away and did not return until two days later, when it came back and did some more talking in crow language, keeping at a safe distance meanwhile. It then went away and never returned.

Social heredity had robbed me of a fine pet! The only consolation I got from the loss of my crow was the thought that it had shown fine sportsmanship by coming back and giving notice of its intention to depart. Many farm hands have left the farm without going to the trouble of this formality.

It is a well-known fact that a fox will prey upon all manner of fowl and small animals with the exception of the skunk. No reason need be stated as to why Mr. Skunk enjoys immunity. A fox may tackle a skunk once, but never twice! For this reason a skunk hide, when nailed to a chicken roost, will keep all but the very young and inexperienced foxes at a safe distance.

The odor of a skunk, once experienced, is never to be forgotten. No other smell even remotely resembles it. It is nowhere recorded that any mother fox ever taught her young how to detect and keep away from the familiar smell of a skunk, but all who are informed on fox lore know that foxes and skunks never seek lodging in the same cave.

But one lesson is sufficient to teach the fox all it cares to know about skunks. Through the Law of Social Heredity, operating via the sense of smell, one lesson serves for an entire lifetime.

———————

A bullfrog can be caught on a fishhook by attaching a small piece of red cloth or any other small red object to the hook and dangling it in front of the frog's nose. That is, Mr. Frog may be caught in this manner, provided he is hooked the first time he snaps at the bait, but if he is poorly hooked and makes a getaway, or if he feels the point of the hook when he bites at the bait but is not caught, he will never make the same mistake again. I spent many hours in stealthy attempt to hook a particularly desirable specimen which had snapped and missed, before learning that but one lesson in social heredity is enough to teach even a humble croaker that bits of red flannel are things to be let alone.

———————

Once I owned a very fine male Airedale dog that caused no end of annoyance by his habit of coming home with a young chicken in his mouth. Each time the chicken was taken away from the dog and he was soundly switched, but to no avail; he continued in his liking for fowl.

For the purpose of saving the dog, if possible, and as an experiment with social heredity, this dog was taken to the farm of a neighbor who had a hen and some newly hatched chickens. The hen was placed in the barn and the dog was turned in with her. As soon as everyone was out of

IS IT NOT STRANGE

THAT WE FEAR MOST

THAT WHICH NEVER HAPPENS?

THAT WE DESTROY OUR INITIATIVE

BY THE FEAR OF DEFEAT,

WHEN, IN REALITY, DEFEAT IS

A MOST USEFUL TONIC AND

SHOULD BE ACCEPTED AS SUCH.

sight the dog slowly edged up toward the hen, sniffed the air in her direction a time or two (to make sure she was the kind of meat for which he was looking), then made a dive toward her. Meanwhile Mrs. Hen had been doing some surveying on her own account, for she met Mr. Dog more than halfway; moreover, she met him with such a surprise of wings and claws as he had never before experienced. The first round was clearly the hen's. But a nice fat bird, reckoned the dog, was not to slip between his paws so easily; therefore he backed away a short distance, then charged again. This time Mrs. Hen lit upon his back, drove her claws into his skin, and made effective use of her sharp bill! Mr. Dog retreated to his corner, looking for all the world as if he were listening for someone to ring the bell and call the fight off until he got his bearings. But Mrs. Hen craved no time for deliberation; she had her adversary on the run and showed that she knew the value of the offensive by keeping him on the run.

One could almost understand her words as she flogged the poor Airedale from one corner to another, keeping up a series of rapid-fire sounds that for all the world resembled the remonstrations of an angry mother who had been called upon to defend her offspring from an attack by older boys.

The Airedale was a poor soldier. After running around the barn from corner to corner for about two minutes he spread himself on the ground as flat as he could and did his best to protect his eyes with his paws. Mrs. Hen seemed to be making a special attempt to peck out his eyes.

The owner of the hen then stepped in and retrieved her—or, more accurately stating it, he retrieved the dog—which in no way appeared to meet with the dog's disapproval.

The next day a chicken was placed in the cellar where the dog slept. As soon as he saw the bird he tucked his tail between his legs and ran for a corner. He never again attempted to catch a chicken. One lesson in social heredity, via the sense of touch, was sufficient to teach him that while chicken chasing may offer some enjoyment, it is also fraught with many hazards.

All these illustrations, with the exception of the first, describe the process of gathering knowledge through direct experience. Observe the marked difference between knowledge gathered by direct experience and that which is gathered through the training of the young by the old, as in the case of the ruffed grouse and her young.

The most impressive lessons are those learned by the young from the old, through highly colored or emotionalized methods of teaching. When the mother grouse spread her wings, stood her feathers on end, shook herself like a man suffering with the palsy, and chattered to her young in a highly excited manner, she planted the fear of humans in their hearts in a manner which they were never to forget.

The term social heredity as used in connection with this lesson, has particular reference to all methods through which a child is taught any idea, dogma, creed, religion, or system of ethical conduct, by its parents or those who may have authority over it, before reaching the age at which it may reason and reflect upon such teaching in its own way; estimating the age of such reasoning power at, let us say, seven to twelve years.

Fear in Middle Age

There are myriad forms of *fear*, but none are more deadly than the fear of poverty and old age. We drive our bodies as if they were slaves because we are so afraid of poverty that we wish to hoard money *for*—*what*—*old age!* This common form of *fear* drives us so hard that we overwork our bodies and bring on the very thing we are struggling to avoid.

What a tragedy to watch men and women drive themselves when they begin to arrive along about the forty-year mile post of life—the age at which they are just beginning to mature mentally. At forty, we are just entering the age in which we are able to see and understand and assimilate the handwriting of Nature, as it appears in the forests and flowing brooks and faces of other adults and little children, yet this devil *fear* drives us so hard that we become blinded and lost in the en-tanglement of a maze of conflicting *desires*. The principle of *organized effort* is lost sight of, and instead of laying hold of Nature's forces that are in evidence all around us, and permitting those forces to carry us to the heights of great achievement, we defy them and they become forces of destruction.

THE POWER OF SELF-CONFIDENCE

Perhaps none of these great forces of Nature are more available for our personal growth and self-improvement than is the principle of autosuggestion, but ignorance of this force is leading the majority of the human race to apply it so that it acts as a hindrance and not as a help.

Following are four examples, arbitrarily two men and two women, that show just how this misapplication of a great force of Nature takes place:

Here is a man who meets with some disappointment; a friend proves false, or a neighbor seems indifferent. Forthwith he decides (through self-suggestion) all people are untrustworthy and all neighbors unappreciative. These thoughts so deeply imbed themselves in his subconscious mind that they color his whole attitude toward others. Go back, now, to what was said in Lesson Two, about the way the dominating thoughts of our minds attract others whose thoughts are similar.

Apply the Law of Attraction and you will soon see and understand why the unbeliever attracts other unbelievers.

Reverse the principle:

Here is a woman who sees nothing but the best there is in all whom she meets. If her neighbors seem indifferent she takes no notice of that fact, for she makes it *her business* to fill her mind with dominating thoughts of optimism and good cheer and faith in others. If people speak to her harshly she speaks back in tones of softness. Through the operation of this same eternal Law of Attraction she draws to herself the attention of people whose attitude toward life and whose dominating thoughts harmonize with her own. Tracing the principle a step further:

Here is a man who has been well schooled and has the ability to render the world some needed service. Somewhere, sometime, he has heard it said that modesty is a great virtue and that to push himself to the front of the stage in the game of life shows egotism. He quietly slips in at the back door and takes a seat at the rear while other players in the game of life boldly step to the front. He remains in the back row because he *fears* "what *they* will say." Public opinion, or that which he believes to be public opinion, has him pushed to the rear and the world hears but little of him. His schooling counts for naught because he is *afraid* to let the world know that he has had it. He is constantly *suggesting to himself* (thus using the great force of autosuggestion to his own detriment) that he should remain in the background lest he be criticized, as if criticism would do him any damage or defeat his purpose.

Here is a woman who was born of poor parents. Since the first day that she can remember, she has seen evidence of poverty. She has heard talk of poverty. She has felt the icy hand of poverty on her shoulders and it has so impressed her that she fixes it in her mind as a curse to which *she must submit.* Quite unconsciously she permits herself to fall victim to the belief "once poor always poor" until that belief becomes the dominating thought of her mind. She resembles a horse that has been harnessed and broken until it forgets that it has the potential power with which to throw off that harness. Autosuggestion is rapidly relegating her to the back of the stage of life. Finally she becomes a *quitter.* Ambition is gone. Opportunity comes her way no longer, or if it does she has not the vision to see it. *She has accepted her fate!* It is a well-established fact that the faculties of the mind, like the limbs of the body, atrophy and wither away if not used. Self-confidence is no exception. It develops when used but disappears if not used.

One of the chief disadvantages of inherited wealth is the fact that it too often leads to inaction and loss of self-confidence. Some years ago a baby boy was born to Mrs. E. B. McLean, in the city of Washington. His inheritance was said to be around $100 million. When this baby was taken for an airing in his carriage it was surrounded by nurses and assistant nurses and detectives and other servants whose duty was to see that no harm befell it. As the years passed by this same vigilance was kept up. This child did not have to dress himself; he had servants who did that. Servants watched over him while he slept and while he was at play. He was not permitted to do anything that a servant could do for him. He had grown to the age of ten years. One day he was playing in the yard and noticed that the back gate had been left open. In all of his life he had never been outside of that gate alone, and naturally that was just the thing that he wished to do. During a moment when the servants were not looking he dashed out at the gate and was run down and killed by an automobile before he reached the middle of the street.

He had used his servants' eyes until his own no longer served him as they might have done had he learned to rely upon them.

Twenty years ago the man to whom I served as secretary sent his two sons away to school. One of them went to the University of Virginia and the other to a college in New York. Each month it was a part of my task to make out a check for $100 for each of these boys. [The 2001 value would be more than $1,800.] This was their pin money, to be spent as they wished. How profitably I remember the way I envied those boys as I made out those checks each month. I often wondered why the hand of fate bore me into the world in poverty. I could look ahead and see how these boys would rise to the high stations in life while I remained a humble clerk.

In due time the boys returned home with their sheepskins. Their father was a wealthy man who owned banks and railroads and coalmines and other property of great value. Good positions were waiting for the boys in their father's employ.

But, twenty years of time can play cruel tricks on those who have never had to struggle. Perhaps a better way to state this truth would be that *time gives those who have never had to struggle a chance to play cruel tricks on themselves!* At any rate, these two boys brought home from school other things besides their sheepskins. They came back with well-developed capacities

YOUR WORK AND MINE

ARE PECULIARLY AKIN; I AM

HELPING THE LAWS OF NATURE

CREATE MORE PERFECT SPECIMENS

OF VEGETATION, WHILE YOU

ARE USING THOSE SAME LAWS,

THROUGH THE LAW OF

SUCCESS PHILOSOPHY, TO CREATE

MORE PERFECT SPECIMENS

OF THINKERS.

—Luther Burbank

for strong *drink—capacities which they developed because the $100 which each of them received each month made it unnecessary for them to struggle.*

Theirs is a long and sad story, the details of which will not interest you, but you will be interested in their *finis.* As this lesson is being written I have on my desk a copy of the newspaper published in the town where these boys lived. Their father has been bankrupted and his costly mansion, where the boys were born, has been placed on the block for sale. One of the boys died of alcohol-related causes and the other one has been confined to a mental health facility.

Not all rich men's sons turn out so unfortunately, but the fact remains, nevertheless, that inaction leads to atrophy and this, in turn, leads to loss of ambition and self-confidence, and without these essential qualities a man will be carried through life on the wings of uncertainty, just as a dry leaf may be carried here and there on the bosom of the stray winds.

Far from being a disadvantage, struggle is a decided advantage, because it develops those qualities that would forever lie dormant without it. Many a man has found his place in the world because of having been forced to struggle for existence early in life. Lack of knowledge of the advantages accruing from struggle has prompted many a parent to say, "I had to work hard when I was young, but I shall see to it that my children have an easy time!" Poor foolish creatures. An "easy" time usually turns out to be a greater handicap than the average young man or woman can survive. There are worse things in this world than being forced to work in early life. Forced idleness is far worse than forced labor. Being forced to work, and forced to do your best, will breed in you temperance and self-control and strength of will and content and a hundred other virtues which the idle will never know.

Not only does lack of the necessity for struggle lead to weakness of ambition and willpower, but, what is more dangerous still, it sets up in a person's mind a state of lethargy that leads to the loss of self-confidence. The person who has quit struggling because effort is no longer necessary is literally applying the principle of autosuggestion, undermining his or her own power of self-confidence. Such a person will finally drift into a frame of mind in which he or she will actually look with contempt upon the person who is forced to carry on.

The human mind, if you will pardon repetition, may be likened to an electric battery. It may be positive or it may be negative. Self-confidence is the quality with which the mind is recharged and made positive.

Let us apply this line of reasoning to salesmanship and see what part self-confidence plays in this great field of endeavor. One of the greatest salesmen this country has ever seen was once a clerk in a newspaper office.

It will be worth your while to analyze the method through which he gained his title as "the world's leading salesman."

He was a timid young man with a more or less retiring sort of nature. He was one of those who believe it best to slip in by the back door and take a seat at the rear of the stage of life. One evening he heard a lecture on the subject of this lesson, self-confidence, and that lecture so impressed him that he left the lecture hall with a firm determination to pull himself out of the rut into which he had drifted.

He went to the business manager of the paper and asked for a position as an advertising salesman and was put to work on a commission basis. Everyone in the office expected to see him fail, as this sort of salesmanship calls for the most positive type of sales ability. He went to his room and made out a list of a certain type of merchants on whom he intended to call. One would think that he would naturally have made up his list of the names of those whom he believed he could sell with the least effort, *but he did nothing of the sort.* He placed on his list only the names of the merchants on whom other advertising solicitors had called without making a sale. His list consisted of only twelve names. Before he made a single call he went out to the city park, took out his list of twelve names, read it over a hundred times, saying to himself as he did so, "You will purchase advertising space from me before the end of the month."

Then he began to make his calls. The first day he closed sales with three of the twelve "impossibilities." During the remainder of the week he made sales to two others. By the end of the month he had opened advertising accounts with all but one of the merchants that he had on the list. For the ensuing month he made no sales, for the reason that he made no calls except on this one obstinate merchant. Every morning when the store opened he was on hand to interview this merchant and every morning the merchant said no. The merchant knew he was not going to buy advertising space, but this young man didn't know it. When the merchant said no the young man did not hear it, but kept right on coming. On the last day of the month, after having told this persistent young man no for thirty consecutive times, the merchant said: "Look here, young man, you have wasted a whole month trying to sell me; now, what I would like to know is this—why have you wasted your time?"

"Wasted my time nothing," he retorted; "I have been going to school and you have been my teacher. Now I know all the arguments that a merchant can bring up for not buying, and besides that I have been drilling myself in self-confidence."

Then the merchant said: "I will make a little confession of my own. I, too, have been going to school, and you have been my teacher. You have taught me a lesson in persistence that is worth money to me, and to show you my appreciation I am going to pay my tuition fee by giving you an order for advertising space."

And that was the way in which the *Philadelphia North American's* best advertising account was brought in. Likewise, it marked the beginning of a reputation that has made that same young man a millionaire. He succeeded because he deliberately charged his own mind with sufficient self-confidence to make that mind an irresistible force. When he sat down to make up that list of twelve names he did something that ninety-nine people out of a hundred would not have done—he selected the names of those whom he believed it would be hard to sell, because he understood that out of the resistance he would meet with in trying to sell them would come strength and self-confidence. He was one of the very few who understand that all rivers and some people are crooked because of following the line of least resistance.

I am going to digress and break the line of thought for a moment to offer a word of advice to spouses and companions.

From having analyzed more than 16,000 people, the majority of whom were married, I have learned something that may be of value.

You have it within your power to send your mate away to his or her work, business, or profession each day with a feeling of self-confidence that will carry him or her successfully over the rough spots of the day and bring him or her home again, at night, smiling and happy. One of my acquaintances of former years married a woman who had a set of false teeth. One day his wife dropped her teeth and broke the plate. The husband picked up the pieces and began examining them. He showed such interest in them that his wife said:

"You could make a set of teeth like those if you made up your mind to do it."

This man was a farmer whose ambitions had never carried him beyond the bounds of his little farm until his wife made that remark. She walked over and laid her hand on his shoulder and encouraged him to try his hand at dentistry. She finally coaxed him to make the start, and today he is one of the most prominent and successful dentists in the state of Virginia. I know him well, for he is my father!

No one can foretell the possibilities of achievement available to the man or woman whose partner supports and encourages bigger and better endeavor. It is your right and your duty to encourage your mate in worthy undertakings until he or she finds an appropriate place in the world. You can induce your mate to put forth greater effort than can any other person in the world. Make your companion believe that nothing within reason is beyond reach and you will have rendered a service that will go a long way toward winning the battle of life.

One of the most successful men in his line in America gives entire credit for his success to his wife. When they were first married she wrote a creed which he signed and placed over his desk. This is a copy of the creed:

I believe in myself. I believe in those who work with me. I believe in my employer. I believe in my friends. I believe in my family. I believe that God will lend me everything I need with which to succeed if I do my best to earn it through faithful and honest service. I believe in prayer and I will never close my eyes in sleep without praying for divine guidance to the end that I will be patient with other people and tolerant with those who do not believe as I do. I believe that success is the result of intelligent effort and does not depend upon luck or sharp practices or double-crossing friends, fellow men, or my employer. I believe I will get out of life exactly what I put into it, therefore I will be careful to conduct myself toward others as I would want them to act toward me. I will not slander those whom I do not like. I will not slight my work no matter what I may see others doing. I will render the best service of which I am capable because I have pledged myself to succeed in life and I know that success is always the result of conscientious and efficient effort. Finally, I will forgive those who offend me because I realize that I shall sometimes offend others and I will need their forgiveness.

Signed . . . .

The woman who wrote this creed was a practical psychologist of the first order. With the influence and guidance of such a marriage partner as a helpmate any man or woman could achieve noteworthy success.

Analyze this creed and you will notice how freely the personal pronoun is used. It starts off with the affirmation of self-confidence,

NO MAN CAN BECOME

A GREAT LEADER OF MEN

UNLESS HE HAS THE MILK

OF HUMAN KINDNESS

IN HIS OWN HEART,

AND LEADS BY SUGGESTION

AND KINDNESS,

RATHER THAN BY FORCE.

which is perfectly proper. You could make this creed your own without developing the positive attitude that would attract people who would aid you in the struggle for success.

This would be a splendid creed for every salesperson to adopt. It might not hurt your chances for success if *you* adopted it. Mere adoption, however, is not enough. You must *practice* it! Read it over and over until you know it by heart. Then repeat it at least once a day until you have literally transformed it into your mental make-up. Keep a copy of it before you as a daily reminder of your pledge to practice it. By doing so you will be making efficient use of the principle of autosuggestion as a means of developing self-confidence. Never mind what anyone may say about your procedure. Just remember that it is your business to succeed, and this creed, if mastered and applied, will go a long way toward helping you.

You learned in Lesson Two that any idea you firmly fix in your subconscious mind, by repeated affirmation, automatically becomes a plan or blueprint which an unseen power uses in directing your efforts toward the attainment of the objective named in the plan.

You have also learned that the principle through which you may fix any idea you choose in your mind is called autosuggestion, which simply means a suggestion that you give to your own mind. It was this principle of autosuggestion that Emerson had in mind when he wrote:

"Nothing can bring you peace but yourself!"

You might well remember that *nothing can bring you success but yourself.* Of course you will need the cooperation of others if you aim to attain success of a far-reaching nature, but you will never get that cooperation unless you vitalize your mind with the positive attitude of self-confidence.

Perhaps you have wondered why a few advance to highly paid positions while others all around them, who have as much training and who seemingly perform as much work, do not get ahead. Select any two people of these two types that you choose, and study them, and the reason why one advances and the other stands still will be quite obvious to you.

You will find that the one who advances *believes in himself or herself.* You will find that belief backed with such dynamic, aggressive action that others know about self-confidence. You will also notice that this self-confidence is contagious; it is impelling; it is persuasive; it attracts others.

You will also find that the one who does not advance shows clearly, by the look on his face, by the posture of his body, by the lack of briskness in his step, by the uncertainty with which he speaks, that he lacks self-confidence. No one is going to pay much attention to the person who has no confidence in himself.

He does not attract others because his mind is a negative force that repels rather than attracts.

In no other field of endeavor does self-confidence or the lack of it play such an important part as in the field of sales, and one does not need to be a character analyst to determine, on first meeting, whether a salesperson possesses this quality of self-confidence. If you have it the signs of its influence are written all over you. You inspire customers with confidence in you and in the goods you are selling the moment you speak.

We come, now, to the point at which you are ready to take hold of the principle of autosuggestion and make direct use of it in developing yourself into a positive and dynamic and self-reliant person. You are instructed to copy the following formula, sign it, and commit it to memory:

Self-Confidence Formula

1. I know that I have the ability to achieve the object of my definite purpose, therefore I demand of myself persistent, aggressive, and continuous action toward its attainment.

2. I realize that the dominating thoughts of my mind eventually reproduce themselves in outward, bodily action and gradually transform themselves into physical reality, therefore I will concentrate my mind for thirty minutes daily upon the task of thinking of the

person I intend to be, by creating a mental picture of this person and then transforming that picture into reality through practical service.

3. I know that through the principle of autosuggestion, any desire that I persistently hold in my mind will eventually seek expression through some practical means of realizing it, therefore I shall devote ten minutes daily to demanding of myself the development of the factors named in the seventeen lessons of this course on the Law of Success.

4. I have clearly mapped out and written down a description of my Definite Purpose in life, for the coming five years. I have set a price on my services for each of these five years; a price that I intend to *earn* and *receive*, through strict application of the principle of efficient, satisfactory service which I will render in advance.

5. I fully realize that no wealth or position can long endure unless built upon truth and justice; therefore *I will engage in no transaction that does not benefit all whom it affects.* I will succeed by attracting to me the forces I wish to use and the cooperation of other people. I will induce others to serve me because I will first serve them. I will eliminate hatred, envy, jealousy, selfishness, and cynicism by developing love for all humanity, because I know that a negative attitude toward others can never bring me success. I will cause others to believe in me because I will believe in them and in myself.

I will sign my name to this formula, commit it to memory, and repeat it aloud once a day with full faith that it will gradually influence my entire life so that I will become a successful and happy worker in my chosen field of endeavor.

Signed . . . .

Before you sign your name to this formula make sure that you intend to carry out its instructions. Back of this formula lies a law that is

IF YOU WANT A THING DONE WELL,

CALL ON SOME BUSY PERSON TO DO IT.

BUSY PEOPLE ARE GENERALLY

THE MOST PAINSTAKING

AND THOROUGH IN ALL THEY DO.

difficult to explain. Psychologists refer to this law as autosuggestion and let it go at that, but you should bear in mind one point about which there is no uncertainty, and that is the fact that whatever this law is it *actually works!*

Another point to be kept in mind is the fact that, just as electricity will turn the wheels of industry and serve mankind in a million other ways, or snuff out life if wrongly applied, so will this principle of auto-suggestion lead you up the mountainside of peace and prosperity, or down into the valley of misery and poverty, according to the application you make of it. If you fill your mind with doubt and unbelief in your ability to achieve, then the principle of autosuggestion takes this spirit of unbelief and sets it up in your subconscious mind as your dominating thought and slowly but surely draws you into the whirlpool of *failure.* But, if you fill your mind with radiant self-confidence, the principle of autosuggestion takes this belief and sets it up as your dominating thought and helps you master the obstacles that fall in your way until you reach the mountaintop of *success.*

THE POWER OF HABIT

Having, myself, experienced all the difficulties that stand in the road of those who lack the understanding to make practical application of this great principle of autosuggestion, let me take you a short way into the principle of habit, through the aid of which you may easily apply the principle of autosuggestion in any direction and for any purpose whatsoever.

Habit grows out of environment; out of doing the same thing or thinking the same thoughts or repeating the same words over and over again. Habit may be likened to the groove on a record, while the human mind may be likened to the needle that fits into that groove. When any habit has been well formed, through repetition of thought or action, the mind has a tendency to attach itself to and follow the course of that habit as closely as the phonograph needle follows the groove in the record.

Habit is created by *repeatedly* directing one or more of the five senses of seeing, hearing, smelling, tasting, and feeling, in a given direction. After habit has been well established it will automatically control and direct our bodily activity, wherein may be found a thought that can be transformed into a powerful factor in the development of self-confidence. The thought is this: *voluntarily, and by force if necessary, direct your efforts and your thoughts along a desired line until you have formed the habit that will lay hold of you and continue, voluntarily, to direct your efforts along the same line.*

The object in writing out and repeating the self-confidence formula is to form the habit of making belief in yourself the dominating thought of your mind until that thought has been thoroughly imbedded in your subconscious mind, through the principle of *habit.*

You learned to write by repeatedly directing the muscles of your arm and hand over certain outlines known as letters, until finally you formed the habit of tracing these outlines. Now you write with ease and rapidity, without tracing each letter slowly. Writing has become a *habit* with you.

The principle of habit will lay hold of the faculties of your mind just the same as it will influence the physical muscles of your body, as you can easily prove by mastering and applying this lesson on self-confidence. Any statement that you repeatedly make to yourself, or any *desire* that you deeply plant in your mind through repeated statement, will eventually seek expression through your physical, outward bodily efforts. The principle of habit is the very foundation upon which this lesson on self-confidence is built, and if you will understand and follow the directions laid down in this lesson you will soon know more about the Law of Habit, from first-hand knowledge, than could be taught you by a thousand such lessons as this.

You have but little conception of the possibilities which lie sleeping within you, awaiting but the awakening hand of vision to arouse you, and you will never have a better conception of those possibilities unless you develop sufficient self-confidence to lift you above the commonplace influences of your present environment.

The human mind is a marvelous, mysterious piece of machinery, a fact of which I was reminded a few months ago when I picked up Emerson's Essays and reread his essay on spiritual laws. A strange thing happened. I saw in that essay, which I had read scores of times previously, much that I had never noticed before. I saw more in this essay than I had seen during previous readings because the unfoldment of my mind since the last reading had prepared me to interpret more.

The human mind is constantly unfolding, like the petals of a flower, until it reaches the maximum of development. What this maximum is, where it ends, or whether it ends at all or not, are unanswerable questions, but the degree of unfoldment seems to vary according to the nature of the individual and the degree to which you keep your mind at work. A mind that is forced or coaxed into analytical thought every day seems to keep on unfolding and developing greater powers of interpretation.

Down in Louisville, Kentucky, lives Mr. Lee Cook, a man who has practically no legs and has to wheel himself around on a cart. In spite of the fact that Mr. Cook has been without legs since birth, he is the owner of a great industry and a millionaire through his own efforts. He has proved that people can get along very well without legs if they have a well-developed self-confidence.

In the city of New York one may see a strong able-bodied and able-headed young man, without legs, rolling himself down Fifth Avenue every afternoon with cap in hand, begging for a living. His head is perhaps as sound and as able to think as the average.

This young man could duplicate anything that Mr. Cook, of Louisville, has done, if *he thought of himself as Mr. Cook thinks of himself.*

Henry Ford owns more millions of dollars than he will ever need or use. Not so many years ago, he was working as a laborer in a machine shop, with but little schooling and without capital. Scores of other men, some of them with better-organized brains than his, worked near him. Ford threw off the poverty consciousness, developed confidence in

YOU CAN ALWAYS

BECOME THE PERSON

YOU WOULD HAVE LIKED TO BE.

himself, thought of success, and attained it. Those who worked around him could have done as well had they *thought* as he did.

Milo C. Jones, of Wisconsin, was stricken down with paralysis a few years ago. So bad was the stroke that he could not turn himself in bed or move a muscle of his body. His physical body was useless, but there was nothing wrong with his brain, so it began to function in earnest, probably for the first time in its existence. Lying flat on his back in bed, Mr. Jones made that brain create a *definite purpose.* That purpose was prosaic and humble enough in nature, but it was *definite* and it was a *purpose,* something that he had never known before.

His *definite purpose* was to make pork sausage. Calling his family around him he told of his plans and began directing them in carrying the plans into action. With nothing to aid him except a sound mind and plenty of *self-confidence,* Milo C. Jones spread the name and reputation of "Little Pig Sausage" all over the United States, and accumulated a fortune besides.

All this was accomplished after paralysis had made it impossible for him to work with his hands.

COMMENTARY

Many more modern examples can also be cited. There is a powerful disease called amyotrophic lateral sclerosis, which is also known as Lou Gehrig's disease. It affects the nerves that control the muscles, causing them to waste away, bringing paralysis and usually death in just a few short years. This condition afflicts the famous physicist, Dr. Stephen Hawking, and has for more than two decades. Dr. Hawking's body is severely limited, but his mind is not. He has taken his mind down incredible roads where he explores the secrets of the universe, studying black holes, quantum physics, even the very nature of time. Dr. Hawking's mind has unfolded to a previously unimagined degree because he made it his habit to develop it.

Peter Leonard seemed to have been dealt a tough hand in life. He had learning disabilities that gave him a very hard time with reading and writing. By the time *he reached middle age, he was divorced and unemployed. But he conceived an idea that came to dominate his mind. He wanted to serve in the New Hampshire legislature. He lost his first campaign and his second. Others would have given up, but Leonard looked at himself and realized that his best chances lay in his own efforts, despite the fact that he had no experience and less money. So for his next campaign, he began going door to door in his district. He met everyone he could, he walked in parades, attended community meetings. He spent just $12 on some posters and $36 on filing fees, and that was the extent of his spending. And Peter Leonard was elected! His path was unusual, but he found it by making a habit of working toward being elected.*

Where *thought* prevails power may be found! Henry Ford has made millions of dollars and is still making millions of dollars each year because *he believed in Henry Ford* and transformed that belief into a *definite purpose* and backed that purpose with a definite plan. The other machinists who worked along with Ford, during the early days of his career, visioned nothing but a weekly pay envelope and that was all they ever got. They demanded nothing out of the ordinary of themselves. If you want to *get more,* be sure to *demand* more of yourself. Notice that this demand is to be made on *yourself.*

There comes to mind a familiar poem whose [unknown] author expressed a great psychological truth:

> *If you think you are beaten, you are;*
> *If you think you dare not, you don't;*
> *If you like to win, but you think you can't,*
> *It is almost certain you won't.*

> *If you think you'll lose you've lost,*
> *For out of the world we find*
> *Success begins with a fellow's will—*
> *It's all in the state of mind.*

If you think you are outclassed, you are—
   You've got to think high to rise.
You've got to be sure of yourself before
   You can ever win a prize.

Life's battles don't always go
   To the stronger or faster man;
But soon or late the man who wins
   Is the man who thinks he can.

It can do no harm if you commit this poem to memory and use it as a part of your working equipment in the development of self-confidence.

Somewhere in your make-up there is a "subtle something" which, if it were aroused by the proper outside influence, would carry you to heights of achievement such as you have never before anticipated. Just as a master player can take hold of a violin and cause that instrument to pour forth the most beautiful and entrancing strains of music, so is there some outside influence that can lay hold of your mind and cause you to go forth into the field of your chosen endeavor and play a glorious symphony of success. No one knows what hidden forces lie dormant within *you*. You, yourself, do not know your capacity for achievement, and you never will know until you come in contact with that particular stimulus which arouses you to greater action and extends your vision, develops your self-confidence, and moves you with a deeper *desire* to achieve.

It is not unreasonable to expect that some statement, some idea, or some stimulating word of this course on the Law of Success will serve as the needed stimulus that will reshape your destiny and redirect your thoughts and energies along a pathway that will lead you, finally, to your coveted goal of life. It is strange, but true, that the most important turning points of life often come at the most unexpected times and in the most unexpected ways. I have in mind a typical example of how some of the seemingly unimportant experiences of life often turn out to be the most important of all, and I am relating this case because it shows, also, what a person can accomplish when he or she awakens to a full understanding of the value of self-confidence. The incident to which I refer happened in the city of Chicago, while I was engaged in the work of character analysis. One day a tramp presented himself at my office and asked for an interview. As I looked up from my work and greeted him he said, "I have come to see the man who wrote this little book," as he removed from his pocket a copy of a book entitled *Self-Confidence*, which I had written many years previously. "It must have been the hand of fate," he continued, "that slipped this book into my pocket yesterday afternoon, because I was about ready to go out there and punch a hole in Lake Michigan. I had about come to the conclusion that everything and everybody, including God, had it in for me until I read this book, and it gave me a new viewpoint and brought me the courage and the hope that sustained me through the night. I made up my mind that if I could see the man who wrote this book he could help me get on my feet again. Now, I am here and I would like to know what you can do for a man like me."

While he was speaking I had been studying him from head to foot, and I am frank to admit that down deep in my heart I did not believe there was anything I could do for him, but I did not wish to tell him so. The glassy stare in his eyes, the lines of discouragement in his face, the posture of his body, the ten days' growth of beard on his face, the nervous manner about this man all conveyed to me the impression that he was hopeless, but I did not have the heart to tell him so; therefore I asked him to sit down and tell me his whole story. I asked him to be perfectly frank and tell me, as nearly as possible, just what had brought him down to the ragged edge of life. I promised him that after I had heard his entire story I would then tell him whether or not I could be of service to him. He related his story, in lengthy detail, the sum and substance of which was this: he had invested his entire fortune in a small manufacturing business. When the world war began in 1914, it was impossible for him to get the raw materials necessary for the operation of his factory, and he therefore failed. The loss of his money broke his heart and so disturbed his mind that he left his wife and children and became a tramp. He had actually brooded over his loss until he had reached the point at which he was contemplating suicide.

After he had finished his story, I said to him: "I have listened to you with a great deal of interest, and I wish that there was something that I could do to help you, but *there is absolutely nothing*."

He became as pale as he will be when he is laid away in a coffin, and settled back in his chair and dropped his chin on his chest as much as to say, "That settles it." I waited for a few seconds, then said:

"While there is nothing that I can do for you, there is a man in this building to whom I will introduce you, if you wish, who can help you regain your lost fortune and put you back on your feet again." These words had barely fallen from my lips when he jumped up, grabbed me by the hands, and said, "For God's sake lead me to this man."

It was encouraging to note that he had asked this "for God's sake." This indicated that there was still a spark of hope within his breast, so I took him by the arm and led him out into the laboratory where my psychological tests in character analysis were conducted, and stood with him in front of what looked to be a curtain over a door. I pulled the curtain aside and uncovered a tall mirror in which he saw himself from head to foot. Pointing my finger at the glass I said:

"There stands the man to whom I promised to introduce you. There is the only man in this world who can put you back on your feet again, and unless you sit down and become acquainted with that man, as you never became acquainted with him before, you might just as well go on over and 'punch a hole' in Lake Michigan, because you will be of no value to yourself or to the world until you know this man better."

He stepped over to the glass, rubbed his hands over his bearded face, studied himself from head to foot for a few moments, then stepped back, dropped his head, and began to weep. I knew that the lesson had

THE ONLY MAN WHO MAKES NO

MISTAKES IS THE MAN WHO NEVER

DOES ANYTHING. DO NOT BE AFRAID

OF MISTAKES PROVIDING YOU DO NOT

MAKE THE SAME ONE TWICE.

—Theodore Roosevelt

been driven home, so I led him back to the elevator and sent him away. I never expected to see him again, and I doubted that the lesson would be sufficient to help him regain his place in the world, because he seemed to be too far gone for redemption. He seemed to be not only *down*, but almost *out*.

A few days later I met this man on the street. His transformation had been so complete that I hardly recognized him. He was walking briskly, with his head tilted back. That old, shifting, nervous posture of his body was gone. He was dressed in new clothes from head to foot. He looked prosperous and he felt prosperous. He stopped me and related what had happened to bring about his rapid transformation from a state of abject failure to one of hope and promise.

"I was just on my way to your office," he explained, "to bring you the good news. I went out the very day that I was in your office, a down-and-out tramp, and despite my appearance I sold myself at a salary of $3,000 a year. *Think of it, man, $3,000 a year!* And my employer advanced me money enough to buy some new clothes, as you can see for yourself. He also advanced me some money to send home to my family, and I am once more on the road to success. It seems like a dream when I think that only a few days ago I had lost hope and faith and courage, and was actually contemplating suicide.

"I was coming to tell you that one of these days, when you are least expecting me I will pay you another visit, and when I do I will be a successful man. I will bring with me a check, signed in blank and made payable to you, and you may fill in the amount because you have saved me from myself by introducing me to myself—that self which I never knew until you stood me in front of that mirror and pointed out the real me."

As that man turned and departed in the crowded streets of Chicago I saw, for the first time in my life, what strength and power and possibility lie hidden in the mind of the man who has never discovered the value of *self-reliance.* Then and there I made up my mind that I, too, would stand in front of that same looking glass and point an accusing finger at myself for not having discovered the lesson which I had helped another to learn. I did stand before that same looking glass, and as I did so I then and there fixed in my mind, as my *definite purpose* in life, the determination to help men and women discover the forces that lie sleeping within them. The book you hold in your hands is evidence that my definite purpose is being carried out.

The man whose story I have related is now the president of one of the largest and most successful concerns of its kind in America, with a business that extends from coast to coast and from Canada to Mexico.

A short while after the incident just related, a woman came to my office for personal analysis. She was then a teacher in the Chicago public schools. I gave her an analysis chart and asked her to fill it out. She had been at work on the chart but a few minutes when she came back to my desk, handed back the chart, and said, "I do not believe I will fill this out." I asked her why she had decided not to fill out the chart and she replied: "To be perfectly frank with you, one of the questions in this chart put me to thinking and I now know what is wrong with me; therefore I feel it unnecessary to pay you a fee to analyze me." With that the woman went away and I did not hear from her for two years. She went to New York City, became a writer of advertising copy for one of the largest agencies in the country, and her income at the time she wrote me was $10,000 a year. [In today's terms this would be about exactly $100,000, though depending on the nature of the work or the company the salary for a similar position might be as little as $60,000 or as much as $200,000.]

This woman sent me a check to cover the cost of my analysis fee, because she felt that the fee had been earned, even though I did not render her the service that I usually render my clients. It is impossible for anyone to foretell what seemingly insignificant incident may lead to an important turning point in one's career, but there is no denying the fact that these "turning points" may be more readily recognized by those who have well-rounded-out confidence in themselves.

One of the irreparable losses to the human race lies in the lack of knowledge that there is a definite method through which self-confidence can be developed in any person of average intelligence. What an immeasurable loss to civilization that young men and women are not taught this known method of developing self-confidence before they complete their schooling, for no one who lacks faith in himself is really educated in the proper sense of the term.

Oh, what glory and satisfaction would be the happy heritage of the man or woman who could pull aside the curtain of *fear* that hangs over the human race and shuts out the sunlight of understanding that self-confidence brings, wherever it is in evidence.

Where *fear* controls, noteworthy achievement becomes an impossibility, a fact which brings to mind the definition of *fear*, as stated by a great philosopher:

"Fear is the dungeon of the mind into which it runs and hides and seeks seclusion. Fear brings on superstition and superstition is the dagger with which hypocrisy assassinates the soul."

In front of the typewriter on which I am writing the manuscripts for this course hangs a sign with the following wording, in big letters:

"Day by day in every way I am becoming more *successful.*"

A skeptic who read that sign asked if I really believed "that stuff" and I replied, "Of course not. All it ever did for me was to help me get out of the coal mines, where I started as a laborer, and find a place in the world in which I am serving upwards of 100,000 people, in whose minds I am planting the same positive thought that this sign brings out; therefore, why should I believe in it?"

As this man started to leave he said: "Well, perhaps there is something to this sort of philosophy, after all, for I have always been afraid that I would be a failure, and so far my fears have been thoroughly realized."

You are condemning yourself to poverty, misery, and failure, or you are driving yourself on toward the heights of great achievement, solely by the thoughts you think. If you *demand* success of yourself and back up

LOVE, BEAUTY, JOY, AND WORSHIP

ARE FOREVER BUILDING,

TEARING DOWN, AND REBUILDING

THE FOUNDATION

OF EACH MAN'S SOUL.

this demand with intelligent action you are sure to win. Bear in mind, though, that there is a difference between *demanding* success and just merely wishing for it. You should find out what this difference is and take advantage of it.

Do you remember what the Bible says about those who have faith as a grain of mustard seed? (Look it up, in the book of Matthew, chapter 13.) Go at the task of developing self-confidence with at least that much faith if not more. Never mind "what *they* will say" because you might as well know that *"they"* will be of little aid to you in your climb up the mountainside of life toward the object of your *definite purpose.* You have within you all the power you need with which to get whatever you want or need in this world, and about the best way to avail yourself of this power is to *believe in yourself.*

"Know thyself, man; know thyself."

This has been the advice of the philosophers all down the ages. When you *really* know yourself you will know that there is nothing foolish about hanging a sign in front of you that reads like this: "Day by day in every way I am becoming more successful," with due apologies to Emile Coue, who made this motto popular. I am not afraid to place this sort of suggestion in front of my desk, and, what is more to the point, I am not afraid to believe that it will influence me so that I will become a more positive and aggressive human being.

More than twenty-five years ago I learned my first lesson in self-confidence building. One night I was sitting before an open fireplace, listening to a conversation between some older men on the subject of capital and labor. Without invitation I joined in the conversation and said something about employers and employees settling their differences on the Golden-Rule basis. My remarks attracted the attention of one of the men, who turned to me, with a look of surprise on his face and said:

"Why you are a bright boy, and if you would go out and get a schooling you would make your mark in the world."

Those remarks fell on fertile ears, even though that was the first time anyone had ever told me that I was bright, or that I might accomplish anything worthwhile in life. The remark put me to thinking, and the more I allowed my mind to dwell upon that thought the more certain I became that the remark had back of it a possibility.

It might be truthfully stated that whatever service I am rendering the world and whatever good I accomplish should be credited to that off-hand remark.

Suggestions such as this are often powerful, and none the less so when they are deliberate and self-expressed. Go back, now, to the self-confidence formula and master it, for it will lead you into the "power-house" of your own mind, where you will tap a force that can be made to carry you to the very top of the ladder of success.

Others will believe in you only when you believe in yourself. They will "tune in" on your thoughts and feel toward you just as you feel to-ward yourself. The Law of Mental Telepathy takes care of this. You are continuously broadcasting what you think of yourself, and if you have no faith in yourself, others will pick up the vibrations of your thoughts and mistake them for their own. Once you understand the Law of Mental Telepathy you will know why self-confidence is the third of the Seventeen Laws of Success.

You should be cautioned, however, to learn the difference between self-confidence, which is based upon sound knowledge of what you know and what you can do, and egotism, which is only based upon what you *wish* you knew or could do. Learn the difference between these two terms or you will make yourself boring, ridiculous, and annoying to people of culture and understanding. Self-confidence is something that should never be proclaimed or announced except through intelligent per-formance of constructive deeds.

If you have self-confidence those around you will discover this fact. Let them make the discovery. They will feel proud of their alertness in having made the discovery, and you will be free from the suspicion of egotism. Opportunity never stalks the person with a highly developed state of egotism, but brickbats and ugly remarks do. Opportunity forms affinities much more easily and quickly with self-confidence than it does with egotism. Self-praise is never a proper measure of self-reliance. Bear this in mind and let your self-confidence speak only through the tongue of constructive service rendered without fuss or flurry.

Self-confidence is the product of knowledge. Know yourself, know how much you know (and how little), why you know it, and how you are going to use it. Four-flushers come to grief, therefore, do not pretend to know more than you actually do know. There's no use of pretense, because any educated person will measure you quite accurately after hearing you speak for three minutes. What you really are will speak so loudly that what you claim you are will not be heard.

If you heed this warning the last few pages of this one lesson may mark one of the most important turning points of your life.

Believe in yourself, but do not *tell* the world what you can do: *Show it!*

DISCONTENTMENT—AN AFTER-THE-LESSON VISIT WITH THE AUTHOR

The marker stands at the entrance gate of life and writes "Poor Fool" on the brow of the wise man and "Poor Sinner" on the brow of the saint.

The supreme mystery of the universe is life! We come here without our consent, from whence we know not! We go away without our consent, whither, we know not!

We are eternally trying to solve this great riddle of *life*, and, for what purpose and to what end?

That we are placed on this earth for a definite reason there can be no doubt by any thinker. May it not be possible that the power that placed us here will know what to do with us when we pass on beyond the Great Divide?

Would it not be a good plan to give the Creator who placed us here on earth credit for having enough intelligence to know what to do with us after we pass on; or, should we assume the intelligence and the ability to control the future life in our own way? May it not be possible that we can cooperate with the Creator very intelligently by assuming to control our conduct on this earth to the end that we may be decent to one another and do all the good we can in all the ways we can during this life, leaving the hereafter to one who probably knows, better than we, what is best for us?

From birth until death the mind is always reaching out for that which it does not possess.

The little child, playing with its toys on the floor, sees another child with a different sort of toy and immediately tries to lay hands on that toy.

Adults continue to pursue what they perceive as bigger, better, and more toys, the more the better.

F. W. Woolworth, the five and ten cent stores king, stood on Fifth Avenue in New York City and gazed upward at the tall Metropolitan Building and said: "How wonderful! I will build one much taller." The crowning achievement of his life was measured by the Woolworth Building. That building stands as a temporary symbol of man's nature to excel the handiwork of other men. *A monument to the vanity of man, with but little else to justify its existence!*

The little ragged newsboy on the street stands, with wide-open mouth, and envies the businessman as he alights from his automobile at the curb and starts into his office. "How happy I would be," the newsboy says to himself, "if I owned a car like that." And, the businessman seated at his desk inside, thinks how happy he would be if he could add another million dollars to his already overswollen bankroll.

The grass is always sweeter on the other side of the fence says the jackass, as he stretches his neck in the attempt to get to it.

Turn a crowd of boys into an apple orchard and they will pass by the nice mellow apples on the ground. The red, juicy ones hanging dangerously high in the top of the tree look much more tempting, and up the tree they will go.

The married man takes a sheepish glance at the ladies on the street and thinks how fortunate he would be if his wife were as pretty as they. Perhaps she is much prettier, but he misses that beauty because—well, because "the grass is always greener on the other side of the fence."

Happiness is always just around the bend; always in sight but just out of reach. Life is never complete, no matter what we have or how much of it we possess. One thing calls for something else to go with it.

You long for a home—just a plain little house sitting off in the edge of the woods. You build it, but it is not complete; you must have shrubbery and flowers and landscaping to go with it. Still it is not complete; you must have a beautiful fence around it, with a graveled driveway.

That calls for a second car and a garage.

All these little touches have been added, but to no avail! The place is now too small. You must have a house with more rooms. The Ford must be replaced by a Cadillac.

On and on the story goes, ad infinitum!

You receive a salary sufficient to keep yourself and your family fairly comfortable. Then comes a promotion and an advance in salary of $1,000 a year. Do you lay the extra $1,000 away in the savings account and continue living as before? You do nothing of the sort. Immediately you must trade the old car in for a new one. A porch must be added to the house. Someone needs a new wardrobe. The table must be set with better food.... At the end of the year are you better off with such an increase? Nothing of the sort! The more you get the more you want, and the rule applies to the millionaire as much as it does to someone with only a few thousand dollars.

A young man selects the girl of his choice, believing he cannot live without her. After he gets her he is not sure that he can live with her. If a man remains a bachelor he wonders why he is so stupid as to deprive himself of the joys of married life. If he marries he wonders how she happened to catch him off guard long enough to "harpoon" him.

And the god of destiny cries out "O fool, O fool! You are damned if you do and you are damned if you *don't.*"

At every crossroad of life the imps of discontentment stand in the shadows of the background, with a grin of mockery on their faces, crying out "Take the road of your own choice! We will get you in the end!"

At last many become disillusioned and begin to learn that happiness and contentment are not of this world. Then begins the search for the password that will open the door to some world of which we know nothing. Surely there must be happiness on the other side of the Great Divide. In desperation his tired, careworn heart turns to religion for hope and encouragement.

But his troubles are not over; they are just starting!

In the midst of sectarian claims and counterclaims we become undecided. Not knowing whether to turn this way or that, we wonder which brand of religion offers the safest passageway, until hope vanishes. As expressed in the Rubayat of Omar Khayyam (in the Fitzgerald translation):

Myself when young did eagerly frequent
Doctor and Saint and heard great argument
About it and about; but evermore
Came out by the same door where in I went.

Always seeking but never finding—this might describe the human struggle for happiness and contentment. We try one religion after another, finally joining the "Big Church" which the world has named the "damned." Our minds become eternal question marks, searching hither and yon for an answer to the questions, "Whence and Whither?"

The worldly hope men set their Hearts upon
Turns Ashes—or it prospers; and anon,
Like Snow upon the Desert's Dusty Face
Lighting a little Hour or two—is gone.

Life is an everlasting question mark!

That which we want most is always in the embryonic distance of the future. Our power to acquire is always a decade or so behind our power to *desire!*

And, if we catch up with the thing we want we no longer want it!

Our favorite author is a hero and a genius until we meet him in person and learn the sad truth that, after all, he is only human. As Emerson wrote, "How often must we learn this lesson? People cease to interest us when we find their limitations. The only sin is limitation. As soon as you once come up with a man's limitations, it is all over with him."

How beautiful the mountain yonder in the distance; but, the moment we draw near it we find it to be nothing but a wretched collection of rocks and dirt and trees.

Out of this truth grew the oft-repeated adage "Familiarity breeds contempt."

Beauty and happiness and contentment are states of mind. They can never be enjoyed except through vision of the afar. The most beautiful painting of Rembrandt becomes a mere smudge of daubed paint if we come too near it.

Destroy the hope of unfinished dreams in a person's heart and he or she is finished.

The moment we cease to cherish the vision of future achievement we are through. Nature has built us so that our greatest and only lasting happiness is that which we feel in the pursuit of some yet unattained object. Anticipation is sweeter than realization. That which is at hand does not satisfy. The only enduring satisfaction is that which comes to the person who keeps alive in his heart the hope of future achievement. When that hope dies write *finis* across the human heart.

Life's greatest inconsistency is the fact that most of that which we believe is not true. Russel Conwell wrote an extremely popular lecture called "Acres of Diamonds." The central idea of the lecture was the statement that one need not seek opportunity in the distance; that opportunity may be found in the vicinity of one's birth. Perhaps! But, how many believe it?

Opportunity may be found wherever one really looks for it, and nowhere else! To most of us the picking looks better on the other side of the fence. How futile to urge one to try out one's luck in the little hometown when it is human nature to look for opportunity in some other locality.

Do not worry because the grass looks sweeter on the other side of the fence. Nature intended it so. Thus does she allure us and groom us for the lifelong task of *growth through struggle.*

SOME MODERN "MIRACLES"

Some people doubt the authenticity of the Bible because they believe that if miracles could be performed over two thousand years ago, before the dawn of science, while the world was still steeped in illiteracy and superstition, it should be just as easy to perform them today.

I have read the Bible very carefully, some parts of it many times; I am convinced that it contains no account of any alleged miracle that has not been more than matched in our times, in the open light of science. Moreover, these modern day miracles are subject to analysis and proof. Any child of average intelligence, above the age of twelve years, may understand the miracles of today, and for this reason I here concern myself about these modern revelations by faith.

The Greatest of All Miracles Is Faith

This is a wonderful age! It is an age of provable miracles.

These are the modern miracles that have impressed me most:

The miracle which Edison performed when, after thousands of temporary failures, he wrested from Nature the secret by which the sound of the human voice may be recorded on a wax record and reproduced perfectly. That miracle was wrought through Edison's *faith*. He had no precedent to guide him. No other person had ever performed such a miracle.

One of the strange things about this miracle is the fact that Edison began at the very outset to experiment with the rudimentary principle and the mechanical apparatus through which the secret of the talking machine was later revealed. The principle was vibration and the apparatus was a tube made of wax that revolved on a cylinder which contacted the point of a needle. Nothing but faith could have enabled Edison to have begun so near the source of the secret which he sought, and nothing but faith could have given him the persistence to stick to his experiments through more than ten thousand failures.

It was faith which enabled Edison to concentrate his mind upon the task which led him through many thousand failures before he created the incandescent lamp with which he harnessed the energy known as electricity and made it serve to light the world.

It was faith which prompted Edison to continue his experiments with the moving picture machine until he made it actually perform the miracle which he must have seen through his own imagination before he even began.

It was faith that sustained the Wright brothers through the years of hazardous experiments before they conquered the air and created a machine that excels, in both speed and endurance, the swiftest bird of the air.

It was faith that prompted Christopher Columbus to set sail on an uncharted sea, in search of a land that, as far as he was concerned, existed nowhere except in his own imagination. Considering the frailties of the little sailing vessels in which he embarked on that momentous voyage, his faith must have been of that variety which enables a person to see the object of his labor already attained even before he begins it.

It was faith that inspired Copernicus to see that portion of a universe which human eyes had never beheld, and at a time in the history of the world when such revelations as those which he wrought through his faith and his crude mechanical equipment might mean his destruction at the hands of his contemporaries who *believed* there were no stars excepting those within range of the human eyes.

It was his faith in a cause that enabled Mahatma Gandhi of India to blend into a single mass the minds of more than two hundred million of his countrymen, every individual of whom would do Gandhi's bidding even though it meant immediate death. No other influence excepting faith could have performed this miracle. Because he has a mind that is capable of sustained faith, Gandhi wields this power passively. Gandhi has proved that faith can accomplish that which trained soldiers and money and implements of warfare cannot achieve.

It was faith that cut the shackles of limitation from the mind of Professor Einstein and revealed to him mathematical principles that the world had not even suspected to exist. No fear-bound mind could have uncovered such a miracle.

It was faith which sustained our own beloved Washington and drove him on to victory in opposition to vastly superior physical forces; a form of faith which was born of his love for freedom for mankind.

The profound principle known as faith is as available to you as it ever was to any human being who has passed this way.

If your world is one of limitation, misery, and want, it is because you have not been quickened to the realization that you have in your own mind a laboratory that is equipped to engender the power of faith.

If we may judge the possibilities of the future by the achievements of the past, the miracles remaining to be uncovered are vastly greater in number and nature than those that have been revealed in the past. It is not yet revealed what our destiny may be.

This is an age of revelation!

Those who believe that the power of revelation passed away with the superstition and ignorance which prevailed a few hundred years ago have but little comprehension of our modern history.

Men like Watt, Whitney, Bell, Howe, Steinmetz, Edison, the Wright brothers, Lee DeForest, Henry Ford, Simon Lake, Arthur Nash, Einstein, and Gandhi are all miracle men. They have removed the horizons of men's minds and discovered unto us new worlds. Ours is a day of miracles; and this is an age of faith.

The world is passing through an experience that will call for many forms of readjustment of human relationships. The real leadership during this period will be found among those who have great capacity for faith. There will be no place in the program of the immediate future for the weaklings and those who still believe that miracles belong only in the age of the dead past, or that they are wrapped up unfathomable mystery. *The miracles of the future will be revealed by science.* The research carried on in the field of science has already uncovered the approach to revelations incomparably greater than any of the past.

Lesson Four

The Habit of Saving

THE ONLY LASTING FAVOR

WHICH THE PARENT

MAY CONFER UPON THE CHILD

IS THAT OF HELPING THE CHILD

TO HELP ITSELF.

Lesson Four

THE HABIT OF SAVING

"Man is a combination of flesh, bone, blood, hair, and brain cells. These are the building materials out of which he shapes, through the Law of Habit, his own peronality."

To ADVISE ONE TO SAVE MONEY WITHOUT describing how to save would be somewhat like drawing the picture of a horse and writing under it, "This is a horse." It is obvious to all that the saving of money is one of the essentials for success, but the big question uppermost in the minds of the majority of those who do not save is:

"How can I do it?"

The saving of money is solely a matter of *habit*. For this reason this lesson begins with a brief analysis of the Law of Habit.

It is literally true that man, through the Law of Habit, shapes his own personality. Through repetition, any act indulged in a few times becomes a habit, and the mind appears to be nothing more than a mass of motivating forces growing out of our daily habits.

When once fixed in the mind a habit voluntarily impels one to action. For example, follow a given route to your daily work, or to some other place that you frequently visit, and very soon the habit has been formed and your mind will lead you over that route without thought on your part. Moreover, if you start out with the intention of traveling in another direction, without keeping the thought of the change in routes constantly in mind, you will find yourself following the old route.

Public speakers have found that the telling over and over again of a story, which may be based upon pure fiction, brings into play the Law of Habit, and very soon they forget whether the story is true or not.

LIMITATION BUILT THROUGH HABIT

Millions of people go through life in poverty and want because they have made destructive use of the Law of Habit. Not understanding either the Law of Habit or the Law of Attraction through which "like attracts like," those who remain in poverty seldom realize that they are where they are as the result of their own acts.

Fix in your mind the thought that your ability is limited to a given earning capacity and you will never earn more than that, because the Law of Habit will set up a definite limitation of the amount you can earn. Your subconscious mind will accept this limitation, and very soon you will feel yourself "slipping" until finally you will become so hedged in by fear of poverty (one of the six basic fears) that opportunity will no longer knock at your door; your doom will be sealed; your fate fixed.

Formation of the habit of saving does not mean that you shall limit your earning capacity; it means just the opposite—that you shall apply this law so that it not only conserves that which you earn, in a systematic manner, but it also places you in the way of greater opportunity and gives you the vision, the self-confidence, the imagination, the enthusiasm, the initiative and leadership actually to increase your earning capacity.

Stating this great law in another way, when, you thoroughly understand the Law of Habit you may insure yourself success in the great game of moneymaking by "playing both ends of that game against the middle."

You proceed in this manner:

First, through the Law of Definite Chief Aim you set up, in your mind, an accurate, definite description of that which you want, including the amount of money you intend to earn. Your subconscious mind takes over this picture which you have created and uses it as a blueprint, chart, or map by which to mold your thoughts and actions into practical plans for attaining the object of your chief aim, or purpose. Through the Law of Habit you keep the object of your Definite Chief Aim fixed in your mind (in the manner described in Lesson Two) until it becomes firmly and permanently implanted there. This practice will destroy the poverty consciousness and set up in its place a prosperity consciousness. You will actually begin to *demand* prosperity, you will begin to expect it, you will begin to prepare yourself to receive it and to use it wisely, thus paving the way or setting the stage for the development of the habit of saving.

Second, having in this manner increased your earning power you will make further use of the Law of Habit by provision, in your written statement of your Definite Chief Aim, for saving a definite proportion of all the money you earn.

Therefore, as your earnings increase, your savings will, likewise, increase in proportion.

By ever urging yourself on and demanding of yourself increased earning power, on the one hand, and by systematically laying aside a definite amount of all your earnings, on the other hand, you will soon reach the point at which you have removed all imaginary limitations from your own mind and you will then be well started on the road toward financial independence.

Nothing could be more practical or more easily accomplished than this.

Reverse the operation of the Law of Habit, by setting up in your mind the fear of poverty, and very soon this fear will reduce your earning capacity until you will be barely able to earn sufficient money to take care of your actual necessities.

The publishers of newspapers could create a panic in a week's time by filling their columns with news items concerning the actual business failures of the country, despite the fact that but few businesses, compared to the total number in existence, actually fail. The so-called "crime waves" are very largely the products of sensational journalism. A single murder case, when exploited by the newspapers of the country, through scare headlines, is sufficient to start a regular wave of similar crimes in various localities.

We are the victims of our habits, no matter who we are or what may be our life calling. Any idea that is deliberately fixed in the mind, or any idea that is permitted to set itself up in the mind, as the result of suggestion, environment, the influence of associates, etc., is sure to cause us to indulge in acts which conform to the nature of the idea.

Form the habit of thinking and talking of prosperity and abundance, and very soon material evidence of these will begin to manifest itself in the nature of wider opportunity and new and unexpected opportunity.

Like attracts like! If you are in business and have formed the habit of talking and thinking about business being bad, business will be bad. One pessimist, providing he is permitted to continue his destructive influence long enough, can destroy the work of half a dozen competent people, and he will do it by setting adrift in the minds of his associates the thought of poverty and failure.

Don't be this type of man or woman.

One of the most successful bankers in the state of Illinois has this sign hanging in his private office:

"We talk and think only of abundance here. If you have a tale of woe please keep it, as we do not want it."

No business firm wants the services of a pessimist, and those who understand the Law of Attraction and the Law of Habit will no more tolerate the pessimist than they would permit a burglar to roam around their place of business, for the reason that one such person will destroy the usefulness of those around him.

In tens of thousands of homes the general topic of conversation is poverty and want, and that is just what they are getting. They think of poverty, they talk of poverty, they accept poverty as their lot in life. They reason that because their ancestors were poor before them they, also, must remain poor.

The poverty consciousness is formed as the result of the habit of thinking of and fearing poverty. "Lo! the thing I had feared has come upon me."

THE SLAVERY OF DEBT

Debt is a merciless master, a fatal enemy of the savings habit.

Poverty, alone, is sufficient to kill off ambition, destroy self-confidence, and destroy hope, but add to it the burden of debt and all who are victims of these two cruel taskmasters are practically doomed to failure.

No one can do his best work, no one can find self-expression in terms that command respect, no one can either create or carry out a definite purpose in life, with heavy debt hanging over his or her head. Someone bound in the slavery of debt is just as helpless as the slave who is bound by ignorance, or by actual chains.

I have a very close friend whose income is $1,000 a month. [Today worth about ten times that amount.] His wife loves "society" and tries to make a $20,000 showing on a $12,000 income, with the result that this poor fellow is usually about $8,000 in debt. Every member of his family has the spending habit, having acquired this from the mother. The children, two girls and one boy, are now of the age when they are thinking of going to college, but this is impossible because of the father's debts. The result is dissension between the father and his children which makes the entire family unhappy and miserable.

YOU ARE A HUMAN MAGNET

AND YOU ARE CONSTANTLY

ATTRACTING TO YOU PEOPLE

WHOSE CHARACTERS

HARMONIZE WITH YOUR OWN.

It is a terrible thing even to think of going through life like a prisoner in chains, bound down and owned by somebody else on account of debts. The accumulation of debts is a habit. It starts in a small way and grows to enormous proportions slowly, step by step, until finally it takes charge of one's very soul.

Thousands of young people start their married lives with unnecessary debts hanging over their heads and never manage to get out from under the load. After the novelty of marriage begins to wear off the married couple begin to feel the embarrassment of want, and this feeling grows until it leads, oftentimes, to open dissatisfaction with one another, and eventually to the divorce court.

People who are bound by the slavery of debt have no time or inclination to set up or work out ideals, with the result that they drift downward with time until they eventually begin to set up limitations in their own minds, and by these they hedge themselves behind prison walls of *fear* and doubt from which they never escape.

No sacrifice is too great to avoid the misery of debt!

"Think of what you owe yourself and those who are dependent upon you and resolve to be no man's debtor," is the advice of one very successful man whose early chances were destroyed by debt. This man came to himself soon enough to throw off the habit of buying that which he did not need and eventually worked his way out of slavery.

Most of those who develop the habit of debt will not be so fortunate as to come to their senses in time to save themselves, because debt is something like quicksand in that it has a tendency to draw its victim deeper and deeper into the mire.

The fear of poverty is one of the most destructive of the six basic fears described in Lesson Three. The person who becomes hopelessly in debt is seized with this poverty fear, his ambition and self-confidence become paralyzed, and they sink gradually into oblivion.

There are two classes of debts, and these are so different in nature that they deserve to be here described, as follows:

- Debts incurred for luxuries that become a dead loss
- Debts incurred in the course of professional or business trading which represent service or merchandise that can be converted back into assets

The first class of debts is the one to be avoided. The second class may be indulged in, providing the one incurring the debts uses judgment and does not go beyond the bounds of reasonable limitation. The moment one buys beyond his or her limitations, that person enters the realm of speculation, and speculation swallows more of its victims than it enriches.

Practically all people who live beyond their means are tempted to speculate with the hope that they may recoup, at a single turn of the wheel of fortune, so to speak, their entire indebtedness. The wheel generally stops at the wrong place and, far from finding themselves out of debt, such people as indulge in speculation are bound more closely as slaves of debt.

The fear of poverty breaks down the willpower of its victims, and they then find themselves unable to restore their lost fortunes, and, what is still more sad, they lose all ambition to extricate themselves from the slavery of debt.

In wartime, millions of men face combat without flinching, knowing that death might overtake them any moment. Those same men, when facing the fear of poverty, often cringe and out of sheer desperation, which paralyzes their reason, sometimes commit suicide.

The person who is free from debt may whip poverty and achieve outstanding financial success, but, if bound by debt, such achievement is but a remote possibility, and never a probability.

Fear of poverty is a negative, destructive state of mind. Moreover, one negative state of mind has a tendency to attract other similar states of mind. For example, the fear of poverty may attract the fear of ill health, and these two may attract the fear of old age, so that the victim finds himself poverty-stricken, in ill health, and actually growing old long before the time when he should begin to show the signs of old age.

Millions of untimely, nameless graves have been filled by this cruel state of mind known as the fear of poverty!

Less than a dozen years ago a young man held a responsible position with the City National Bank, of New York City. Through living beyond his income he contracted a large amount of debts which caused him to worry until this destructive habit began to show up in his work and he was dismissed from the bank's service.

He secured another position, at less money, but his creditors embarrassed him so that he decided to resign and go away into another city, where he hoped to escape them until he had accumulated enough money to pay off his indebtedness. Creditors have a way of tracing debtors, so very soon they were close on the heels of this young man, whose employer found out about his indebtedness and dismissed him from his position.

He then searched in vain for employment for two months. One cold night he went to the top of one of the tall buildings on Broadway and jumped off. Debt had claimed another victim.

COMMENTARY

As you read Hill's comments about debt and poverty the stories may seem melodramatic, and you may feel that they don't bear much relationship to conditions in your world. People's sense of responsibility and personal obligation has changed, and financial debt no longer has the taint about it that it had in Hill's day. After all, the America Hill was writing about was before the crash of '29 and the Great Depression that followed. It was before the modern stock market, anti-trust laws, the FTC, and the Federal Reserve, well before credit cards, and light years before e-commerce and dot-com billionaires.

The times have indeed changed, but the changing social mores have not altered the basic principle of success. The tales that Hill tells may be from another era, *but as was stated earlier, the philosophy those stories convey has made more mil-lionaires than any other philosophy. Those stories inspired people to succeed during the Great Depression, through the Second World War, and they were the touchstone for many who made America boom during the fifties and the sixties. It was those same stories and the philosophy behind them that made some of the most successful entrepreneurs of the baby boom generation, and for those who look past the words and learn the lessons, it will be the making of the new millennium millionaires.*

MASTER THE FEAR OF POVERTY

To whip the fear of poverty one must take two very definite steps, pro-viding one is in debt. First, quit the habit of buying on credit, and follow this by gradually paying off the debts that you have already incurred.

Being free from the worry of indebtedness you are ready to revamp the habits of your mind and redirect your course toward prosperity. Adopt, as a part of your Definite Chief Aim, the habit of saving a reg-ular proportion of your income, even if this be no more than a penny a day. Very soon this habit will begin to lay hold of your mind and you will actually get joy out of saving.

Any habit may be discontinued by building in its place some other and more desirable habit. The spending habit must be replaced by the saving habit by all who attain financial independence.

Merely to discontinue an undesirable habit is not enough, as such habits have a tendency to reappear unless the place they formerly occu-pied in the mind is filled by some other habit of a different nature.

The discontinuance of a habit leaves a hole in the mind, and this hole must be filled up with some other form of habit or the old one will return and claim its place.

Throughout this course many psychological formulas, which the student has been requested to memorize and practice, have been de-scribed. You will find such a formula in Lesson Three, the object of which is to develop self-confidence.

These formulas may be assimilated so they become a part of your mental machinery, through the Law of Habit, if you will follow the instructions for their use which accompany each of them.

It is assumed that you are striving to attain financial independence. The accumulation of money is not difficult after you have once mastered the fear of poverty and developed in its place the habit of saving.

I would be greatly disappointed to know that any student of the course got the impression from anything in this or any of the other lessons that success is measured by dollars alone.

However, money does represent an important factor in success, and it must be given its proper value in any philosophy intended to help people in becoming useful, happy, and prosperous.

The cold, cruel, relentless truth is that in this age of materialism a person is no more than so many grains of sand, which may be blown helter-skelter by every stray wind of circumstance, unless entrenched behind the power of money!

Genius may offer many rewards to those who possess it, but the fact still remains that genius without money with which to give it expression is but an empty, skeletonlike honor.

The person without money is at the mercy of the person who has it!

And this goes, regardless of the amount of ability one may possess or one's training native genius or natural gifts.

There is no escape from the fact that people will weigh you very largely in the light of bank balances, no matter who you are or what you can do. The first question that arises, in the minds of most people, when they meet a stranger, is, "How much money has he?" If he has money he is welcomed into homes and business opportunities are thrown his way. All sorts of attention are lavished upon him. He is a prince, and as such is entitled to the best of the land.

But if his shoes are run down at the heels, his clothes are not pressed, his collar is dirty, and he shows plainly the signs of impoverished finances,

WHO TOLD YOU

IT COULDN'T BE DONE?

AND, WHAT GREAT ACHIEVEMENT

HAS HE TO HIS CREDIT

THAT ENTITLES HIM TO USE

THE WORD "IMPOSSIBLE"

SO FREELY?

woe be his lot, for the passing crowd will step on his toes and blow the smoke of disrespect in his face.

These are not pretty statements, but they have one virtue: *they are true!*

This tendency to judge people by the money they have, or their power to control money, is not confined to any one class of people. We all have a touch of it, whether we recognize the fact or not.

Thomas A. Edison is one of the best-known and most respected inventors in the world, yet it is no misstatement of facts to say that he would have remained a practically unknown, obscure personage had he not followed the habit of conserving his resources and shown his ability to save money.

Henry Ford never would have got to first base with his "horseless carriage" had he not developed, quite early in life, the habit of saving. Moreover, had Mr. Ford not conserved his resources and hedged himself behind their power, he would have been swallowed up by his competitors or those who covetously desired to take his business away from him, long, long years ago.

Many of us have gone a very long way toward success, only to stumble and fall, never again to rise, because of lack of money in times of emergency. The mortality rate in business each year, due to lack of reserve capital for emergencies, is stupendous. To this one cause are due more of the business failures than to all other causes combined!

Reserve funds are essential in the successful operation of business!

Likewise, savings accounts are essential to success on the part of individuals. Without a savings fund the individual suffers in two ways: first, by inability to seize opportunities that come only to the person with some ready cash, and, second, by embarrassment due to some unexpected emergency calling for cash.

It might be said, also, that the individual suffers in still a third respect by not developing the habit of saving, through lack of certain other qualities essential for success which grow out of the practice of the habit of saving.

The nickels, dimes, and pennies that the average person allows to slip through his fingers would, if systematically saved and properly put to work, eventually bring financial independence.

Through the courtesy of a prominent building and loan association the following table has been compiled, showing what a monthly saving of $5, $10, $25, or $50 will amount to at the end of ten years. These figures are startling when one comes to consider the fact that the average person spends from $5 to $50 a month for useless merchandise or so-called "entertainment."

The making and saving of money is a science, yet the rules by which money is accumulated are so simple that anyone may follow them. The main prerequisite is a willingness to subordinate the present to the future, by eliminating unnecessary expenditures for luxuries.

A young man, who was earning only $20 a week as chauffeur for a prominent New York banker, was induced by his employer to keep an accurate account of every cent he spent for one week. The following is an itemized list of his expenses:

Cigarettes	$0.75
Chewing gum	$0.30
Soda fountain	$1.80
Cigars for associates	$1.50
Moving picture show	$1.00
Shaves, including tips	$1.60
Newspaper, daily and Sunday	$0.22
Shoe shines	$0.30
	$7.47
Board and room	$12.00
Money on hand	$0.53
	$20.00

THE AMAZING WAY YOUR MONEY GROWS

Save $5 a Month (Only 17 cents a day)

	Amount Saved	Profit [at about 7% interest]	Savings Plus Profits	Withdrawal Value
1st year	$60.00	$4.30	$64.30	$61.30
2nd year	$120.00	$16.55	$136.00	$125.00
3rd year	$180.00	$36.30	$216.30	$191.55
4th year	$240.00	$64.00	$304.00	$216.20
5th year	$300.00	$101.00	$401.00	$338.13
6th year	$360.00	$140.00	$500.00	$414.75
7th year	$420.00	$197.10	$617.00	$495.43
8th year	$480.00	$157.05	$737.50	$578.32
9th year	$540.00	$324.95	$864.95	$687.15
10th year	$600.00	$400.00	$1000.00	$1000.00

Save $10 a Month (Only 33 cents a day)

	Amount Saved	Profit [at about 7% interest]	Savings Plus Profits	Withdrawal Value
1st year	$120.00	$8.60	$128.60	$122.60
2nd year	$240.00	$33.11	$273.11	$250.00
3rd year	$360.00	$72.60	$432.60	$383.10
4th year	$480.00	$128.00	$608.00	$520.40
5th year	$600.00	$202.00	$802.00	$676.25
6th year	$720.00	$280.00	$1000.00	$829.50
7th year	$840.00	$394.20	$1234.20	$990.85
8th year	$960.00	$514.10	$1474.10	$1156.64
9th year	$1080.00	$649.90	$1729.90	$1374.30
10th year	$1200.00	$800.00	$2000.00	$2000.00

Save $25 a Month (Only 83 cents a day)

	Amount Saved	Profit [at about 7% interest]	Savings Plus Profits	Withdrawal Value
1st year	$300.00	$21.50	$321.50	$306.50
2nd year	$600.00	$82.75	$682.75	$625.00
3rd year	$900.00	$181.50	$1081.50	$957.75
4th year	$1200.00	$320.00	$1520.00	$1301.00
5th year	$1500.00	$505.00	$2005.00	$1690.63
6th year	$1800.00	$700.00	$2500.00	$2073.75
7th year	$2100.00	$985.50	$3085.50	$2477.13
8th year	$2400.00	$1285.25	$3685.25	$2891.60
9th year	$2700.00	$1624.75	$4324.75	$3435.75
10th year	$3000.00	$2000.00	$5000.00	$5000.00

Save $50 a Month (Only $1.66 a day)

	Amount Saved	Profit [at about 7% interest]	Savings Plus Profits	Withdrawal Value
1st year	$600.00	$43.00	$643.00	$613.00
2nd year	$1200.00	$165.00	$1365.00	$1250.00
3rd year	$1800.00	$363.00	$2163.00	$1915.50
4th year	$2400.00	$640.00	$3040.00	$2602.00
5th year	$3000.00	$1010.00	$4010.00	$3381.25
6th year	$3600.00	$1400.00	$5000.00	$4147.50
7th year	$4200.00	$1971.00	$6171.00	$4954.25
8th year	$4800.00	$2570.50	$7370.00	$5783.20
9th year	$5400.00	$3249.50	$8649.50	$6871.50
10th year	$6000.00	$4000.00	$10,000.00	$10,000.00

EVERY FAILURE,

EVERY ADVERSITY,

EVERY HEARTACHE

MAY BE A BLESSING IN DISGUISE

PROVIDING IT SOFTENS

THE ANIMAL PORTION

OF OUR NATURE.

These figures tell a tragic story which might as well apply to thousands of other people as to the young man who kept this account. His actual savings out of $20 were only 53 cents. He spent $7.47 for items, every one of which could have been greatly reduced, and most of which could have been eliminated entirely. In fact, by shaving himself and shining his own shoes, he could have saved every cent of the $7.47.

COMMENTARY

Wayne Wagner and Al Winnikoff, authors of Millionaire, *make a similar point in modern terms. They argue for investment in index funds, which are relatively secure and typically increase in value at a rate of more than 10 percent per year. They work backwards from the goal of saving a million dollars.*

Current age	Years to a million dollars at age 65	Monthly investment required	Daily investment required
25	40	$179	$5.97
30	35	$292	$9.73
35	30	$481	$16.03
40	25	$805	$28.63
45	20	$1382	$46.07
50	15	$2491	$83.03

Now turn to the table made up by the building and loan association and observe what the saving of $7.47 a week would amount to. Suppose the amount this young man actually saved had been only $25 a month; the saving would have increased to the snug sum of $5,000 by the end of the first ten years.

The young man in question was twenty-one years old at the time he kept this expense account. By the time he reached the age of thirty-one years he could have had a substantial amount in the bank had he saved

$25 a month, and this saving would have brought him many opportunities that would have led directly to financial independence.

Some who are short-sighted, pseudo-philosophers are fond of pointing to the fact that no one can become rich merely by saving a few dollars a week.

This may be true enough, as far as the reasoning goes (which is not very far) but the other side of the story is that the saving of even a small sum of money places one in position where, oftentimes, this small sum may enable one to take advantage of business opportunities which lead directly and quite rapidly to financial independence.

The table on page 265, showing what a saving of $5 a month will amount to at the end of ten years, should be copied and pasted on your mirror, where it will stare you in the face every morning when you get up and every night as you retire, providing you have not already acquired the habit of systematic saving of money. This table should be reproduced, in letters and figures an inch tall, and placed on the walls of every public school throughout the land, where it might serve as a constant reminder to all school children of the value of the savings habit.

COMMENTARY

A modern example would look something like this: let us consider the example of Terry, a twenty-six-year-old professional who is earning the very solid amount of $36,000 a year. Terry's monthly financial picture is as follows:

Income:	$3,000	
Outgo:		
	Taxes	$900
	Food	$200
	Rent and bills	$750
	Car payment	$200
	Car insurance	$100

Gas	$100
New clothes	$150
Credit card bills	$150
Student Loan	$200
"Spending Money"	$250
Total outgo:	$3,000

Terry is saving nothing. It seems impossible, with a car and an apartment and a professional wardrobe to keep up, let alone a college loan and a big credit card debt, which is how Terry pays for things like birthday gifts, vacations, car repairs, and new stereo equipment. That $380 spending money vanishes on lunches, dinners out, soap and shampoo, and other little things. How could Terry ever get ahead?

Terry has made some poor choices. The down payment on the new car lease emptied his savings account, and car insurance is steep. A good appearance can be important to success, but Terry has long since established a good basic wardrobe. Worse, with a credit card balance of more than $4,000, Terry is paying more than $600 each year in interest, more than $50 a month. A cheaper apartment alone would provide enough money to pay off half the credit card debt in a year, saving another $300. The car lease is, unfortunately, an obligation Terry is locked into for two years, at the end of which time he will have to take out a new lease or purchase the car for several thousand dollars.

Terry decides to bite the bullet and moves into a cheaper apartment, freeing up $200 monthly. Half of that goes to credit card bills, and the remainder is used to pay cash for purchases that otherwise would have been charged. Additionally, Terry decides to set aside $20 each week—not a large amount, but for Terry, an important beginning.

At the end of a year, Terry will be only $1,200 in debt to credit card companies and able to retire that debt completely in six months more. At the end of that same year, Terry will have more than $1,000 in the bank. After the liberating moment when the last credit card bill is paid, there will be an extra $250 each month. But instead of spending that newly available cash, Terry will be in the grip of the saving habit and will devote all of it to savings, socking away $4,040 over the next twelve months.

Assuming the continuance of that annual savings of $4,040, there will be more than $10,500 in the bank by Terry's thirtieth birthday. Assuming just 3 percent growth and the annual savings contribution, Terry will reach the age of forty with more than $55,000. Having a healthy nest egg to fall back on is a great antidote to the fear of poverty, making it much easier to develop the self-confidence you need to pursue your Definite Chief Aim. How much easier would it be for you to take a risk if you knew that you had $55,000 backing you up?

Some years ago, before giving serious thought to the value of the savings habit, I made a personal account of the money that had slipped through my fingers. The amount was so alarming that it resulted in the writing of this lesson, and adding the habit of saving as one of the Seventeen Laws of Success.

Following is an itemized statement of this account:

Inherited, invested in automobile supply business with a friend who lost the entire amount in one year.	$4,000
Extra money earned from sundry writing for magazines and newspapers, all spent uselessly.	$3,600
Earned from training 3,000 salesmen, with the aid of the Law of Success philosophy, invested in a magazine that was not a success because there was no reserve capital back of it.	$30,000
Extra money earned from public addresses, lectures, etc., all of which was spent as it came in.	$3,400
Estimated amount that could have been saved during a period of ten years out of regular earnings, at the rate of only $50 a month.	$6,000
	$47,000

This amount, had it been saved and invested as received, in building and loan associations or in some other manner that would have earned compound interest, would have grown into the sum of $94,000 at the time this lesson is being written.

I have never been a victim of any of the usual habits, such as gambling, drinking, and excessive entertaining. It is almost unbelievable that someone whose habits of living are reasonably moderate could spend $47,000 within a little over ten years without having anything to show for the money, but it can be done!

I recall one occasion when the president of a large corporation sent me a check for $500 for an address I delivered at a banquet given to the employees, and I distinctly recall what went through my mind when I opened the letter and saw the check. I had wanted a new automobile and this check was exactly the amount required for the first payment. I had it spent before it had been in my hands thirty seconds.

Perhaps this is the experience of the majority of people. They think more of how they are going to *spend* what they have than they do about ways and means of *saving*. The idea of saving, and the self-control and self-sacrifice which must accompany it, is always accompanied by thoughts of an unpleasant nature, but oh, how it does thrill one to think of *spending*.

There is a reason for this, and that reason is the fact that most of us have developed the habit of spending while neglecting the habit of saving, and any idea that frequents the human mind but seldom is not as welcome as that which frequents it often.

In truth, the habit of saving can be made as fascinating as the habit of spending, but not until it has become a regular, well-grounded, systematic habit. We like to do that which is often repeated, which is but another way of stating what the scientists have discovered, that we are victims of our habits.

The habit of saving money requires more force of character than most people have developed, for the reason that saving means self-denial and sacrifice of amusements and pleasures in scores of different ways.

For this very reason one who develops the savings habit acquires, at the same time, many of the other needed habits which lead to success: especially self-control, self-confidence, courage, poise, and freedom from fear.

COMMENTARY

Though some people spend a great deal of money, it does not mean they are rich. In The Millionaire Next Door, *Thomas J. Stanley and William Danko reveal that spending is something that most wealthy people avoid. Their research shows that:*

- *More than 80 percent of America's millionaires accumulated their own wealth—they did not inherit it.*
- *Most millionaires do not live in fancy neighborhoods but in the houses they owned when they began to accumulate their fortunes.*
- *Most millionaires drive mid-sized American cars, not fancy imports, and one out of three of them always buys used cars.*
- *The average millionaire has an income of just over $130,000—their real wealth comes from their habit of saving 20 percent of their income.*

In short, most millionaires are not actors or Fortune 500 CEOs or baseball players pulling down millions of dollars a season. They are people earning good but not fantastic incomes, who have made a habit of saving.

HOW MUCH SHOULD YOU SAVE?

The first question that will arise is, "How much should one save?" The answer cannot be given in a few words, for the amount one should save depends upon many conditions, some of which may be within one's control and some of which may not be.

Generally speaking, a salaried worker should apportion his or her income about as follows:

Savings Account	20 percent
Living: Clothes, Food, and Shelter	50 percent
Education	10 percent
Recreation	10 percent

Life Insurance	10 percent
	100 percent

The following, however, indicates the approximate distribution, which the average person actually makes of his income:

Savings Account	NOTHING
Living: Clothes, Food, and Shelter	60 percent
Education	0 percent
Recreation	35 percent
Life Insurance	5 percent
	100 percent

An experienced analyst has stated that he could tell very accurately, by examining anyone's personal monthly budget, what sort of a life that person is living. Moreover, the analyst will get most of his information from looking at the "recreation" item. This, then, is a figure to be watched as carefully as the greenhouse keeper watches the thermometer that controls the life and death of his plants.

Nothing in this lesson is intended as a sermon on morality, or on any other subject. We are here dealing with cold facts which, to a large extent, constitute the building materials out of which success may be created.

However, this is an appropriate place to state some facts which have such a direct bearing on the subject of achieving success that they cannot be omitted without weakening this entire course in general and this lesson in particular.

I am speaking not as a reformer! Nor am I preaching morals, as this field of useful endeavor is quite well covered by others who are able workers. What is here stated, therefore, is intended as a necessary part of a course of philosophy whose purpose is to mark a safe road over which one may travel to honorable achievement.

CAREFUL ANALYSIS OF 178 MEN

WHO ARE KNOWN TO BE SUCCESSFUL

DISCLOSED THE FACT

THAT ALL HAD FAILED

MANY TIMES BEFORE ARRIVING.

COMMENTARY

In the following section Napoleon Hill goes on at length citing examples of people spending their money on bootleg alcohol instead of saving. The editors have chosen to include these examples in this new edition as a short lesson in human nature. As you read the following section, in your mind, replace the word liquor *with the words* drugs, video games, lottery tickets, *or any other current fad or fashion. No doubt you just experienced Hill's stories from 1927 suddenly becoming as contemporary as today's headlines.*

During the year 1926 I was in partnership with the late Don R. Mellett, who was, at that time, the publisher of the *Canton* (Ohio) *Daily News.* Mr. Mellett became interested in the Law of Success philosophy because it offered, as he believed, sound counsel to young men and young women who really wish to get ahead in life. Through the pages of the *Daily News* Mr. Mellett was conducting a fierce battle against the underworld forces of Canton. With the aid of detectives and investigators, some of whom were supplied by the Governor of Ohio, Mr. Mellett and I gathered accurate data concerning the way most of the people in Canton were living.

In July 1926, Mr. Mellett was assassinated. During the investigation into crime conditions in Canton all reports came to my office, and the data described following are, therefore, absolutely accurate.

A teller in a bank, whose salary was $150 a month, was spending an average of $75 a month for liquor, and in addition to this unpardonable waste of money, out of a salary which was none too great at most, he was traveling at a pace and with a crowd which meant ruin for him later on.

The superintendent of a large manufacturing plant, whose salary was $5,000 a year, and who should have been saving at least $125 a month, was actually saving nothing. His bootlegger's bill averaged $150 a month.

A policeman whose income was $160 a month was spending over $400 a month on dinner parties at a nearby roadhouse. Where he got the difference between his legitimate income and his actual expenditures is a question that reflects no particular credit on the policeman.

A young man who was attending high school was spending large sums for liquor. The actual amount was not obtainable for the reason that he paid cash as he got the liquor, and the bootlegger's records did not, therefore, disclose the actual amount. Later this boy's parents had him locked up "to save him from himself." It was found that he was stealing money from a savings fund kept by his mother, somewhere about the house. He had stolen and spent more than $300 of this money when discovered.

A few years ago I set up a lecture bureau in forty-one high schools, where I lectured once a month during the entire school season. The principals of these high schools stated that less than 2 percent of the students showed any tendency toward saving money, and an examination through the aid of a questionnaire prepared for that purpose disclosed the fact that only 5 percent of the students, out of a total of 11,000 of high-school age, believed that the savings habit was one of the essentials for success.

COMMENTARY

According to the 1999 EBRI Youth and Money Survey, 64 percent of students say they do not know as much about money as they should. Even among students who say they do a very good job of managing their money 49 percent think they should know more.

It is no wonder the rich are becoming richer and the poor are becoming poorer!

We are all victims of *habit!*

Unfortunately for most of us, we are reared by parents who have no conception whatsoever of the psychology of habit, and, without being aware of their fault, most parents aid and abet their offspring in the development of the spending habit by overindulgence with spending money, and by lack of training in the habit of saving.

The habits of early childhood cling to us all through life.

Fortunate, indeed, is the child whose parents have the foresight and the understanding of the value, as a character builder, of the habit of saving, to inculcate this habit in the minds of their children.

It is a training that yields rich rewards.

Give the average person a $100 windfall and what will become of it? Why, the lucky person will begin to cogitate on how to spend the money. Dozens of things that are needed, or perceived as necessary, will flash into that person's mind, but it is a rather safe bet that it will never occur to the recipient (unless he or she has acquired the savings habit) to make this $100 the beginning of a savings account. Before night comes the $100 will be spent, or at least a decision will have been made on how to spend it, thus adding more fuel to the already too bright flame of the habit of spending.

We are ruled by our habits!

It requires force of character, determination, and power of firm decision to open a savings account and then add to it a regular, if small, portion of all subsequent income.

There is one rule by which anyone may determine, well in advance, whether or not financial freedom and independence which is so universally desired is attainable, and this rule has absolutely nothing to do with the amount of one's income.

The rule is that if you follow the systematic habit of saving a definite proportion of all money you earn or receive in other ways, you are practically sure to place yourself in a position of financial independence. If you save nothing, you are *absolutely sure never to be financially independent*, no matter how much your income may be.

The one and only exception to this rule is that someone who does not save might possibly inherit such a large sum of money that he or she could not spend it, or might inherit it under a trust which would protect it, but these eventualities are rather remote; so much so, in fact, that you cannot rely upon such a miracle happening to you.

ALL SALES PEOPLE

WILL DO WELL TO REMEMBER

THAT NO ONE WANTS ANYTHING

THAT SOMEONE ELSE

IS TRYING TO GET RID OF.

I enjoy a rather close acquaintance with many hundreds of people throughout the United States and in some foreign countries. For nearly twenty-five years I have been watching many of these acquaintances, and know, therefore, from actual experience, how they live, why some of them have failed while others have succeeded, and the *reasons for both failure and success.*

This list of acquaintances covers men who control hundreds of millions of dollars, and actually own many millions that they have acquired. Also men who have had millions of dollars, all of which passed through their fingers and they are now penniless.

For the purpose of showing the student of this philosophy just how the Law of Habit becomes a sort of pivotal point on which success or failure turns, and exactly why no one can become financially independent without developing the habit of *systematic saving*, the living habits of some of these many acquaintances will be described.

We will begin with a complete history, in his own words, of a man who made a million dollars in the field of advertising, but who was left with nothing to show for his efforts. This story first appeared in *The American Magazine*, and it is here reprinted through the courtesy of the publishers of that publication.

The story is true, in every respect, and it has been included as a part of this lesson because the author of the story, Mr. W. C. Freeman, is willing to have his mistakes made public with the hope that others may avoid them. (The following is reprinted by courtesy of *The American Magazine.* Copyright, The Crowell Publishing Company, 1927.)

A SAD BUT TRUE STORY

"I Have Made a Million Dollars but I Haven't Got a Cent"

While it is embarrassing, yes, humiliating, publicly to confess to an outstanding fault that has made a good deal of a mess of my life today, nevertheless I have decided to make this confession for the good it may do.

I am going to make a clean breast of how I let slip through my fingers all the money I have earned thus far in my lifetime, which approximates one million dollars. This amount I made through my work in the field of advertising, except a few thousand dollars I earned up to twenty-five years of age by teaching in country schools and by writing news letters to some country weeklies and daily newspapers.

Maybe one lone million does not seem a lot of money in these days of many millions and even billions; but it is a big sum of money, just the same. If there are any who think to the contrary, let them count a million. I tried to figure out the other night how long it would take to do so. I found I could count an average of one hundred a minute. On this basis it would take me twenty days of eight hours each, plus six hours and forty minutes on the twenty-first day to do the stunt. I doubt very much if you or I were given an assignment to count one million one-dollar bills, upon the promise that all of them would be ours at the end of that time, that we could complete it. It would probably drive us mad—and a lot of use the money would be to us then, wouldn't it?

Let me say at the outset of my story that I do not regret, not for one minute, that I spent 90 percent of the money I made. To wish any of this 90 percent back at this time would make me feel that I would have denied much happiness to my family and to many others.

My only regret is that I spent all of my money, and more besides. If I had today the 10 percent I could have saved easily, I would have one hundred thousand dollars safely invested, and no debts. If I had this money I would feel really and truly that I was rich; and I mean just this, for I have never had a desire to accumulate money for money's sake.

Those schoolteaching and newspaper-correspondence days of mine brought some cares and responsibilities, but they were met optimistically.

I married at the age of twenty-one with the full approval of parents on both sides, who believed thoroughly in the doctrine preached by Henry Ward Beecher, that "early marriages are virtuous marriages."

Just one month and one day after I was married my father met a tragic death. He was suffocated by coal gas. Having been an educator all his life—and one of the best—he had not accumulated any money.

When he passed out of our family circle it was up to all of us to pull together and get along somehow, which we did.

Apart from the void left in our home by my father's death (my wife and I and my mother and only sister lived together), we had a joyful life, despite the fact that it was a tight squeeze to make ends meet.

My mother, who was exceptionally talented and resourceful (she had taught school with my father until I was born), decided to open our home to a married couple, old friends of the family. They came to live with us and their board helped to pay expenses. My mother was known far and wide for the wonderful meals she served. Later on, two well-to-do women friends of the family were taken into our home, thus increasing our revenue.

My sister helped very substantially by teaching a kindergarten class, which met in the big living room of our home; my wife contributed her share to the household by taking charge of the sewing and mending.

Those were very happy days. Nobody in the household was extravagant or had any extravagant tendencies except perhaps myself, for I was always inclined to be free with money. I liked to make gifts to the family and to entertain friends.

THINK WELL BEFORE YOU SPEAK

BECAUSE YOUR WORDS

MAY PLANT THE SEED OF

EITHER SUCCESS OR FAILURE

IN THE MIND OF

SOME OTHER PERSON.

When the first baby came into our home—a boy—we all thought heaven had opened its doors to us. My wife's parents, who took the keenest and deepest interest in our affairs, and who were always ready to lend a helping hand, were equally happy over the coming of their first grandchild. My brother-in-law, much older than my wife, and a bachelor, could not understand at first the joy we all felt; but even he began to strut around like a proud peacock after a while. What a difference a baby makes in a home!

I am injecting these details into my story merely to emphasize how the early days of my life were lived. I had no opportunity to spend much money, and yet I had as much happiness in those days as I have ever had since.

The strange thing about it all is that the experience of those days did not teach me the value of money. If anybody ever had a practical lesson to guide him in his future, I certainly had it.

But let me tell you how this early experience affected me. The birth of my son inspired me to do something that would make more money than I was getting at teaching school and in writing for newspapers. I did not want my wife, mother, and sister to feel that they would have to continue indefinitely to do their part in sustaining the household. Why should a fellow, big and strong and healthy as I have always been, and with a reasonable amount of ability, be content to remain a spoke in the wheel? Why shouldn't I be the whole wheel, as far as providing for the family was concerned?

Following my desire to make more money, I took on the selling of books in addition to teaching and writing for newspapers. This earned for me quite a little extra money. Finally, I gave up teaching and concentrated on selling books, and writing for newspapers.

My bookselling took me to Bridgeton, New Jersey. It was here that I got my first real start in making money. I had to be away from home a great deal to do this work, but the sacrifice was worthwhile. I earned enough money in a few weeks to send more money home than I had contributed to the household in any year from my school teaching and newspaper correspondence. After combing the territory in the Bridgeton zone, I became interested in a newspaper in that city, the *Morning Star*. It seemed to me that the editor and publisher of this paper needed a helper. I called on him and told him so. He said, "Heavens, young man, how can I hire you? I am not earning enough money to pay for my own living!"

"That's just it," said I. "I believe together we can make the *Star* a success. I'll tell you what I'll do:

"I'll work for you for one week for one dollar a day. At the end of the week, if I have made good, I'll expect you to pay me three dollars a day for the second week; and then, if I continue to do well, I'll expect you to pay me six dollars a day for the third week, and will continue from then on until the paper makes enough money to pay me fifty dollars a week."

The owner agreed to my proposition. At the end of two months, I was being paid fifty dollars a week, which in those days was considered a big salary. I began to feel that I was well on my way toward making money—but all I wanted it for was to make my family more comfortable. Fifty dollars a week was just four times as much as I had made teaching school.

My job on the *Star* embraced editorial writing (not very brilliant), reporting (just ordinary), the writing and selling of advertisements (fairly successful), proof reading, bill collecting, and so forth. It kept me humping six days a week; but I could stand it, for I was strong and healthy, and, besides, the work was very interesting. I also contributed correspondence to the *New*

York Sun, Philadelphia Record, and the *Trenton* (N.J.) *Times,* which brought me in an average of one hundred and fifty dollars a month, for this was a good news territory.

I learned a lesson on the *Star* that eventually shaped the course of my life. I found out that there is a great deal more money to be earned by selling advertising for newspapers than in writing for them. Advertising brings grist to the mill.

I put over one advertising stunt on the *Star*—a write-up of the south Jersey oyster industry, paid for by the oyster men—that brought in three thousand dollars cash, which the publisher divided with me fifty-fifty. I had never seen so much money at one time in all my life. Think of it! Fifteen hundred dollars—25 percent more than I had made in two years of school teaching and odd tasks.

Did I save this money or any part of it? I did not. What was the use? I could do so much with it to make my wife, boy, mother, and sister happy that I let it go far easier than I had made it.

But would it not have been a fine thing if I had put this money away for a rainy day?

My work in Bridgeton attracted the attention of Sam Hudson, New Jersey correspondent of the *Philadelphia Record,* who was a shining example of that type of newspapermen whose greatest pleasure in life is doing things for others.

Sam told me that it was time for me to get located in a big city. He thought I had it in me to make good. He said he would get me a job in Philadelphia. He did, and I moved with my wife and baby to Germantown. I was given charge of the advertising department of the *Germantown* (Philadelphia) *Gazette,* a weekly newspaper.

At the start I did not make as much money as I had earned in Bridgeton, because I had to give up my newspaper correspondence. The news for this section was covered by other correspondents. But very soon I was making 25 percent more money. The *Gazette* increased its size three times to accommodate its advertising, and each time I received a very substantial increase in salary.

In addition to this, I was given a job to gather social news for the Sunday edition of the *Philadelphia Press*. Bradford Merrill, managing editor of that newspaper, now a very important New York newspaper executive, assigned me a big territory to cover. This kept me busy every night in the week except Saturdays. I was paid five dollars a column; but I averaged seven columns every Sunday, which made me thirty-five dollars a week extra.

It was more money for me to spend, and I spent it. I did not know anything about budgeting my expenses. I just let it go as it came. I did not have time, or thought I hadn't, to watch my step in spending.

A year later I was invited to join the advertising staff of the *Philadelphia Press*, a big opportunity for a young man, for I got wonderful training under the management of William L. McLean, now the owner of the *Philadelphia Evening Bulletin*. I still retained my job as gatherer of social news—so my income was just about the same as I had been making in Germantown.

But before long my work attracted the attention of James Elverson, Sr., publisher of the old *Saturday Night* and *Golden Days*, who had just purchased the *Philadelphia Inquirer*. I was offered and accepted the advertising management of this newspaper.

This meant a big increase in my income. And soon afterward there came a happy increase in my family, the birth of a daughter. Then I was able to do what I had longed to do since the birth of my son. I got the family together again under one roof—my wife and two babies, my mother and sister. At last I was able to relieve my mother of any cares or responsibilities, and never again did she have either as long as she lived. She died in her eighty-first year, twenty-five years after my father's death. I shall never forget her last words to me: "Will, you have never caused me a moment's worry since you were born, and I could not have had more than you have given me had I been the Queen of England."

I was making at this time four times more money than my father had made as superintendent of public schools in my hometown of Phillipsburg, New Jersey.

All the money, however, passed out of my pockets as easily as water flows through a sieve. Expenses increased with every increase in my income, which is the habit, I suppose, with most people. There was no sane reason, though, for letting my expenses go beyond my income, which I did. I found myself piling up debts, and from this time on I was never out of debt. I did not worry about my debts, though, for I thought I could pay them off at any time. It never occurred to me—not until fully twenty-five years later—that debt eventually would bring upon me not only great anxiety and unhappiness, but that I would lose friends and credit as well.

But I must pat myself on the back for one thing: I was giving full rein to my big fault—spending money as fast as I made it, often faster; but I never shirked my work. I was always trying to find more things to do, and I always found them. I spent very little time with my family. I would go home to dinner every night and romp with the babies until their bedtime, then I would return to the office and often work.

So the years went by. Another daughter arrived. Presently I wanted my daughters to have a pony and cart, and I wanted my son to have a riding horse. Then I thought I needed a team to take me around with the family. I got them all. Instead of one horse and a carry-all, or perhaps a team, which would have been sufficient for our needs and something we could have afforded,

I AM THANKFUL FOR THE ADVERSITIES

THAT HAVE CROSSED MY PATHWAY,

FOR THEY HAVE TAUGHT ME

TOLERANCE, SYMPATHY,

SELF-CONTROL, PERSEVERANCE

AND SOME OTHER VIRTUES

I MIGHT NEVER HAVE KNOWN.

I had to have a stable, with all that goes with it. This outfit cost me nearly one-fourth of my annual income.

Then I took up golf. This was in my forty-first year. I went at my play the same as I went at my work—put my whole heart in it. I learned to play pretty well. My son and elder daughter played with me, and they learned to play well, too.

It was necessary that my younger daughter should spend the winter in the South and summers in the Adirondacks; but instead of her mother going with her alone, I felt it would be fine if the son and other daughter went along with them. This arrangement was carried out. They went to Pinehurst, North Carolina, every winter and to expensive resorts in the Adirondacks or in New Hampshire in the summer.

All this took a great deal of money. My son and elder daughter were keen about golf and spent a lot of money on it. I also disbursed quite a little on golf courses around New York. Between the three of us we won 80 prizes, most of which are now in storage. I sat down one day and calculated what these prizes had cost me. I discovered that each trophy had cost me $250 or a total of $45,000 over a period of fifteen years, an average of $3,000 a year. Ridiculous, wasn't it?

I entertained lavishly at my home. Montclair folks thought I was a millionaire. I frequently invited groups of businessmen to have a day of golf at the club, and then to have dinner with me in the evening. They would have been satisfied with a plain home dinner, but, no, I must serve them an elaborate affair staged by a famous caterer. These dinners never cost less than ten dollars a plate, which did not include the money spent for music while they were dining. I had a quartet come to the house. Our dining room comfortably seated twenty people, and it was filled to capacity many times.

It was all very lovely, and I was glad to be their host. In fact, I was very happy over it. I never stopped to think how rapidly I was piling up debts. The day came when they began to bother me a lot. I had entertained so many guests at the golf club one month, paying for luncheons, cigars, and greens fees, that my bill was four hundred and fifty dollars. This attracted the attention of the directors of the club, who were all good friends of mine and very much interested in my welfare. They made it their business to tell me that I was spending entirely too much money, and they wished for my sake that I could check my expenses.

This gave me a bit of a jolt. It made me think seriously long enough to get rid of my horses and traps—at a big sacrifice, of course. I gave up our home and moved back to the city; but I did not leave any unpaid bills in Montclair. I borrowed the money to pay them. It was always easy for me to get all the money I wanted, despite my well-known financial shortcomings.

Here are two sidelights on my experience during my "flaring forties."

Besides spending money foolishly and perhaps recklessly, I loaned it with equal abandon. In cleaning out my desk at home before moving to the city I looked over a package of due bills, the total of which was over forty thousand dollars. That was money handed out to just anybody who came along. I tore them all up; but I realized that if I had that money in hand I wouldn't owe a dollar.

One of the prosperous businessmen I had entertained many times and who in turn had entertained me, said to me: "Billy, I've got to stop going on outings with you. You spend entirely too much money for me. I can't keep up with you."

Think of that coming from a man who was making more money than I was! It should have struck home, but it didn't. I went on spending just the same, and foolishly thinking that I was having a good time, and with no thought of the future. This man is now one of the vice presidents of one of New York's greatest financial institutions, and is reported to be worth many millions of dollars.

I should have taken his advice.

In the fall of 1908, after my disastrous experience of six months in another line of business following my resignation from the Hearst organization, I resumed newspaper work as advertising manager of the *New York Evening Mail.* I had known Henry L. Stoddard, editor and owner, back in the Philadelphia days, when he was political correspondent for the *Press.*

Despite the fact that I was bothered by debts, I did the best work of my life on the *Evening Mail,* and made more money during the five years I was associated with it than I had ever made before. Moreover, Mr. Stoddard gave me the privilege of syndicating advertising talks, which ran in his paper for one thousand consecutive publication days, and earned for me more than fifty-five thousand dollars.

Mr. Stoddard was very generous in many other ways, and frequently paid me special sums of money for doing what he considered unusual things in the way of developing business. During this period, I was so deeply in debt that, in order to keep things moving as smoothly as possible, but without retrenching in the slightest way in my expenses, I borrowed money from Peter to pay Paul and from Paul to pay Peter. That item of fifty-five thousand dollars earned from syndicating advertising talks would have more than paid all my debts and left a nice nest egg besides. But all of it was spent as easily as though I hadn't a care in the world.

In 1915 I went on my own in the advertising business. From that time until the spring of 1922 my fees ran into very big figures. I was still making more money than I ever did, and was spending it just as fast as I made it, until finally my friends got tired of making me loans.

If I had shown the slightest inclination to curb my expenses to the extent of only 10 percent, these wonderful men would have been willing to divide fifty-fifty with me, letting me pay them 5 percent of it and saving 5 percent. They did not care so much about the return of the money they had loaned me, as that they wanted to see me pull myself together.

The crash in my affairs came five years ago. Two friends who had stood by me loyally became impatient, and told me frankly that I needed a drastic lesson. They gave it to me all right. I was forced into bankruptcy, which nearly broke my heart. I felt that every person I knew was pointing the finger of scorn at me. This was very foolish. While there was comment, it was not at all unfriendly. It was expressive of keen regret that a man who had attained so much prestige in his profession, and had earned so much money, should have allowed himself to get into financial difficulties.

Proud and sensitive to the core, I felt the disgrace of bankruptcy so keenly that I decided to go to Florida, where I had once done a special piece of work for a client. It seemed to me to be the coming El Dorado. I figured that maybe I could make sufficient money in a few years so that I could return to New York, not only with a competency but with enough to pay all my debts in full. For a time it looked as though I would realize this ambition; but I was caught in the big real estate collapse. So here I am back in the old town where I once had big earning power and hundreds of friends and well wishers.

It has been a strange experience.

One thing is certain: I have learned my lesson at last. I feel sure that opportunities will come my way to redeem myself, and that my earning power will be restored to me.

And when that time comes I know that I shall be able to live as well as I ever did, on 40 percent of my income. Then I shall divide the remaining 60 percent into two parts, setting aside 30 percent to pay my creditors and 30 percent for insurance and savings.

If I allowed myself to feel depressed over my past, or filled my mind with worries, I would not be capable of carrying on the fight to redeem myself.

Besides, I would be ungrateful to my Maker for having endowed me with wonderful health all my life. Is there any greater blessing?

I would be ungrateful to the memory of my parents, whose splendid training has kept me anchored pretty safely to moral standards. Slipping from moral moorings is infinitely more serious, in the end, than slipping from the thrift standard.

I would lack appreciation for the encouragement and support I have had in generous measure from hundreds of businessmen and to many good friends who helped me build a fine reputation in my profession.

These memories are the sunshine of my life. And I shall use them to pave the way to my future achievement.

With abundance of health, unfaltering faith, unflagging energy, unceasing optimism, and unbounded confidence that a man can win his fight, even though he commences late in life to realize the kind of fight he must make—is there anything but death to stop him?

Mr. Freeman's story is the same as that which might be told by thousands of others who save nothing, with the exception that the amounts of their incomes would vary. The manner of living, the way the money was spent, and why, as told in Mr. Freeman's narrative, show the way the spender's mind works.

FORTUNATE IS THE PERSON

WHO HAS LEARNED THAT

THE MOST CERTAIN WAY TO GET

IS TO FIRST GIVE,

THROUGH SOME SORT

OF USEFUL SERVICE.

The installment plan of buying has become so common, and it is so easy to purchase practically anything one desires, that the tendency to spend out of proportion to one's income is rapidly increasing. This tendency must be curbed by the person who has made up his mind to gain financial independence.

It can be done by anyone who is willing to try.

There is no virtue in keeping up with the pace set by neighbors when this means sacrifice of the habit of saving a regular part of one's income. It is far better, in the long run, to be considered a bit behind the times than it is to go along through youth, into the days of maturity, and finally into old age, without having formed the habit of systematic saving.

It is a common practice today for families to purchase automobiles on monthly payments which involve too great an expenditure compared to their income. If you have a Ford income you have no business purchasing a more expensive car. You should curb your desires and content yourself with a Ford. Many people spend their entire incomes, and often go into debt besides, because they maintain automobiles out of keeping with their incomes. This common practice is fatal to success as far as financial independence may be considered a part of success, in thousands of instances.

It is better to sacrifice during the age of youthfulness, than it is to be compelled to do so during the age of maturity, as all who have not developed the habit of saving generally have to do.

There is nothing quite so humiliating, that carries such great agony and suffering, as poverty in old age when personal services are no longer marketable, and one must turn to relatives or to charitable institutions for existence.

A budget system should be maintained by every person, both the married and the single, but no budget system will work out if the person trying to keep it lacks the courage to cut expenses on such items as those of entertainment and recreation. If you feel so weak in willpower that you think it necessary to "keep up with the Joneses" with whom you associate socially, and whose income is greater than your own, or who spend all of their income foolishly, then no budget system can be of service to you.

I AM THANKFUL THAT

I WAS BORN POOR—

THAT I DID NOT

COME INTO THIS WORLD

BURDENED BY THE WHIMS

OF WEALTHY PARENTS,

WITH A BAG OF GOLD

AROUND MY NECK.

Forming the savings habit means that, to some extent at least, you must seclude yourself from all except a well-selected group of friends who enjoy you without elaborate entertaining on your part.

To admit that you lack the courage to trim down your expenditures so that you can save money, even if only a small amount, is the equivalent of admitting at the same time a lack of the sort of character which leads to success.

It has been proved times too numerous to be mentioned that people who have formed the habit of saving money are always given preference in positions of responsibility; therefore, the saving of money not only adds advantages in the nature of preferred employment and a larger bank account, but it also increases the actual earning capacity. Any businessman will prefer to employ a person who saves money regularly, not because of the mere fact that such person saves money, but because of the characteristics possessed by such a person which make him or her more efficient.

It should be a common practice for all business houses to require all employees to save money. This would be a blessing to thousands of people who would not otherwise have the willpower to form the savings habit.

Henry Ford has gone a very long way, perhaps as far as is expedient, to induce his employees not only to save their money, but to spend what they do spend wisely, and to live sanely and economically. The manager who induces his employees to form the habit of saving is a practical philanthropist.

COMMENTARY

The smart course is to resolve to save a certain percentage of every check that comes to you. This is called "paying yourself first." While 20 percent may seem to be daunting, it will become easier to manage as you experience the excitement of watching your savings grow. If your current situation absolutely will not allow you to set aside 20 percent, select another amount, even just 5 percent. Out of every

$1,000, this is just $50, but repeat that 5 percent savings ten times and you will have $500. Isn't the notion of having $500 tucked away appealing?

You will find that as you watch your savings grow, you will feel a sense of self-confidence. You will realize that you are capable of saving. "What would happen," you will ask, "if I were saving 10 percent, or even 15 percent?" Soon 20 percent will seem far more attainable.

You should strive to reach a point where you have at least three months' take-home pay in your savings account. This will provide you with an important cushion should some unexpected difficulty occur. Even better, a year's worth of living ex-penses set aside will bring you an incredible sense of freedom.

If you have nothing more in the bank than what it will take to get you through next week, this will seem an enormous goal to you. Even by setting aside 20 percent of your income, you will still need almost five years to reach this level of savings. But if you do nothing, in five years you will still be as strapped for cash as you are today.

Perhaps your friends will wonder why you are driving the same car, or why you haven't gone on a Caribbean vacation. Perhaps they will tell you stories about their new satellite television system or the skiing in Aspen. The fear of criticism may as-sail you in such times, but if these people are measuring you solely by how extrav-agantly you spend your money, perhaps they aren't the best of friends.

Avoid the temptation of boasting about your savings activities. Unless you are embarking on a business relationship, this is no one else's concern. It's too easy to find yourself the butt of dumb jokes about being a skinflint or the target of a so-called friend who comes, hat in hand, for a loan that you will never see repaid.

Learn more about what you can do with your savings. There are many good guides to money management.

One reason for accumulating savings is that it can be very useful to you in pur-suing your Definite Chief Aim. When the time comes to embark upon such a pursuit, be sure to hold back a part of your savings. Few people leap to success in a single, smooth movement. There will be surprises and probably some setbacks along the way. Keeping a cushion ready gives you the resiliency to bounce back from disap-pointment and take advantage of the lessons it has taught you.

Your commitment to the habit of saving will prepare you to embrace and use all the lessons of the Law of Success.

OPPORTUNITIES THAT COME TO THOSE
WHO HAVE SAVED MONEY

A few years ago a young man came to Philadelphia from the farming district of Pennsylvania and went to work in a printing plant. One of his fellow workmen owned some shares in a building and loan company and had formed the habit of saving $5 a week, through this association. This young man was influenced by his associate to open an account with the building and loan company. At the end of three years he had saved $900. The printing plant for which he worked got into financial difficulty and was about to fail. He came to the rescue with his $900, which he had saved in small amounts, and in return was given a half interest in the business.

By inaugurating a system of close economy he helped the business to pay off its indebtedness, and today he is drawing out of it, as his half of the profits, a little better than $25,000 a year.

This opportunity never would have come, or, if it had, he would not have been prepared to embrace it, had he not formed the habit of saving money.

When the Ford automobile was perfected, during the early days of its existence, Henry Ford needed capital to promote the manufacture and sale of his product. He turned to a few friends who had saved up a few thousand dollars, one of whom was Senator Couzens. These friends came to his rescue, put in a few thousand dollars with him, and later drew out millions of dollars in profits.

When Woolworth first started his five and ten cent stores plan he had no capital, but he turned to a few friends who had saved, by the closest sort of economy and great sacrifice, a few thousand dollars. These friends staked him and later they were paid back hundreds of thousands of dollars in profits.

Van Heusen (the famed shirt manufacturer) conceived the idea of producing a semi-soft collar for men. His idea was sound, but he had not a cent to promote it. He turned to a few friends who had only a few hundred dollars, who gave him a start, and the collar made each of them wealthy.

The men who started the El Producto Cigar business had but little capital, and what they did have was money they had saved from their small earnings as cigar makers. They had a good idea and knew how to make a good cigar, but the idea would have died aborning had they not saved a little money. With their meager savings they launched the cigar, and a few years later they sold out their business to the American Tobacco Company for $8,000,000.

Back of practically every great fortune one may find, as its beginning, a well-developed habit of saving money.

John D. Rockefeller was an ordinary bookkeeper. He conceived the idea of developing the oil business, which was then not even considered a business. He needed capital, and because he had developed the habit of saving, and had thereby proved that he could conserve the funds of other people, he had no difficulty in borrowing what money he needed. It may be truthfully stated that the real basis of the Rockefeller fortune is the habit of saving money that Mr. Rockefeller developed, while working as a bookkeeper at a salary of $40 a month.

James J. Hill was a poor young man, working as a telegrapher at a salary of $30 a month. He conceived the idea of the Great Northern Railway System, but his idea was out of proportion to his ability to finance. However, he had formed the habit of saving money, and on the meager salary of $30 a month had saved enough to enable him to pay his expenses on a trip to Chicago, where he interested capitalists in financing his plan. The fact that he, himself, had saved money on a small salary was considered good evidence that he would be a safe man to trust with other people's money.

Most people in business will not trust another person with their money unless that person has demonstrated an ability to take care of his own and use it wisely. The test, while it is often embarrassing to those who have not formed the habit of saving, is a very practical one.

A young man who worked in a printing plant in the city of Chicago wanted to open a small print shop and go into business for himself. He went to a printing supply house manager and made known his wants, saying he desired credit for a printing press and some type and other small equipment.

The first question asked by the manager was: "Have you saved any money of your own?"

He had! Out of his salary of $30 a week he had saved $15 a week regularly for nearly four years. He got the credit he wanted. Later on he got more credit, until today he has built up one of the most successful printing plants in the city of Chicago. His name is George B. Williams.

Many years after this incident, I became acquainted with Mr. Williams, and at the end of the war, in 1918, I went to Mr. Williams and asked for credit amounting to many thousands of dollars, for the purpose of publishing the *Golden Rule Magazine*. The first question asked was:

"Have you formed the habit of saving money?" Despite the fact that all the money I had saved was lost in the war, the mere fact that I had actually formed the savings habit was the real basis on which I got credit for upward of $30,000.

There are opportunities on every corner, but they exist only for those who have ready money, or who can command money because they have formed the habit of saving, and developed the other characteristics which go with the formation of the savings habit known by the general term of character.

The late J. P. Morgan once said he would rather loan $1,000,000 to a man of sound character, who had formed the habit of saving money, than he would $1,000 to a man without character, who was a spendthrift.

Generally speaking, this is the attitude which the world takes toward all those who save money.

It often happens that a small savings account of no more than two or three hundred dollars is sufficient to start one on the highway to

LOVE AND JUSTICE

ARE THE REAL ARBITERS

OF ALL DISPUTES.

GIVE THEM A CHANCE

AND YOU WILL NO LONGER

WANT TO DEFEAT

A BROTHER SOJOURNER

BY THE WAYSIDE OF LIFE.

financial independence. A few years ago a young inventor invented a household article which was unique and practical. He was handicapped, as inventors so often are, because he did not have the money to market his invention. Moreover, not having formed the savings habit he found it impossible to borrow money through banking sources.

His roommate was a young machinist who had saved $200. He came to the inventor's aid with this small sum of money and had enough of the articles manufactured to give them a start. They went out and sold, from house to house, the first supply, then came back and had another supply made up, and so on, until they had accumulated (thanks to the thrift and savings ability of the roommate) a capital of $1,000. With this, plus some credit they secured, they bought the tools for manufacturing their own product.

The young machinist sold his half interest in the business, six years later, for $250,000. He never would have handled this much money during his entire life had he not formed the habit of saving, which enabled him to come to the rescue of his inventor friend.

This case might be multiplied a thousand times, with but slight variation as to details, as it is fairly descriptive of the beginning of many great fortunes that have been made and are now in the making, in the United States.

COMMENTARY

There may be times when you find that even having saved money, it is difficult to persuade others to back you, simply because your vision is greater than theirs. Women entrepreneurs, unfortunately, have often had this experience. But a small savings account of no more than a few thousand dollars can be enough to get you started. Mary Kay Ash started her cosmetics company with $5,000 of her own money. Lillian Vernon began with $2,000 she had saved. They created opportunities by their habit of saving.

It may seem like a sad, cruel fact, but it is a *fact* nonetheless, that if you have no money, and have not developed the habit of saving, you are out of luck as far as availing yourself of the opportunity to make money is concerned.

It can do no harm to repeat—in fact it should be repeated over and over again—that the real start of nearly all fortunes, whether great or small, is the formation of the habit of saving money!

Get this basic principle firmly founded in your mind and you will be well on the road toward financial independence!

It is a sad sight to see someone well along in years, who is self-sentenced to the wearisome treadmill of hard labor because he or she has neglected to form the habit of saving money, yet there are millions of such men and women, of all ages and types, living in the United States alone, today.

The greatest thing in life is *freedom!*

There can be no real freedom without a reasonable degree of financial independence. It is a terrible thing to be compelled to be at a certain place, at a certain task (perhaps a task which one does not like) for a certain number of hours every working day of the week, for a whole lifetime. In some ways this is the same as being in prison, since one's choice of action is always limited. It is really no better than being in prison with the privilege of a "trustee," and in some ways it is even worse because the person who is imprisoned has escaped the responsibility of providing a place to sleep, something to eat, and clothes to wear.

The only hope of escape from this lifelong toil which curtails freedom is to form the habit of saving money, and then live up to that habit, no matter how much sacrifice it may require. There is no other way out for millions of people, and unless you are one of the rare exceptions this lesson and all these statements of fact are meant for *you*, and apply to you!

Neither a borrower, nor a lender be;
For loan oft loses both itself and friend,
And borrowing dulls the edge of husbandry.
This above all: to thine own self be true,
And it must follow, as the night the day,
Thou canst not then be false to any man.

—SHAKESPEARE